Kings & Queens
of England & Scotland

Kings & Queens
of England & Scotland

Allen Andrews

with an introduction
by *Dulcie M. Ashdown*

Marshall Cavendish

Published by Marshall Cavendish Books Limited
58 Old Compton Street
London W1V 5PA

First printing 1976
This printing 1985

Printed and bound by Grafiche Editorali Padane S.p.A.,
Cremona, Italy

ISBN 0 85685 136 1

Introduction

It has often been remarked that story-telling is the most powerful tool of the teacher. In history, stories of brave men and fascinating women survive in our memories long after the hard-learned facts and abstract concepts of government or social and economic evolution have faded. Centuries after the power of the world's great empires has dwindled, when their cities stand in ruins and their artifacts are in fragments, their glories can still be evoked through their rich legacy of stories. The stories of the lives of Britain's kings and queens make compelling reading on their own account, but they also serve to illustrate the progress of British history as no formal analysis of trends and developments could do.

'Might is right' was the first principle of monarchy: in primitive societies the bravest warrior, he who could win the most land and wealth in battle, could force himself on his peers as their leader. The many tribal chiefs of ancient Britain in time gave place to the rules of the several kingdoms within Anglo-Saxon England. Eventually, as the result of a national effort against the common threat of the Danish invasions, one man, Alfred of Wessex, proved that he could rule effectively over the whole of England.

For centuries after the lifetime of Alfred, the modern principle of hereditary 'primogeniture' (the succession of the crown from father to eldest son, and to a daughter only in default of a male heir) was not established. When a king died, his young children might be passed over in favour of an older man, a seasoned warrior who could command the loyalty of the majority—although almost invariably these men were themselves members of the royal family. It was not until more than a century after the Norman conquest that the principle of direct succession was accepted.

Traditionally, medieval kings ruled through the advice and support of their great nobles, and when they either ignored such counsel or allowed one faction to dominate their government, they could expect drastic consequences: Edward II, Richard II and Henry VI were murdered for such failings. And from the thirteenth century onwards the Commons of England, in Parliament, asserted ever more urgently their right to share in national decision-making—largely through their sole right to vote taxation to the royal government or withhold it. Charles I so infuriated his subjects by his outrageous demands for personal power that they were goaded into a rebellion potent enough to put an end to monarchic government for more than a decade. When James II flagrantly tried to impose unpopular policies on his kingdom, his subjects forced him to flee for his life, and the next monarchs received the crown only after consenting to abide by certain limitations on their power framed by Parliament. It was this settlement which became

the basis of subsequent rules, written and tacit, which now govern the power of the monarchy. Today Britain has a 'constitutional' monarchy: Queen Elizabeth II has no right to frame legislation, to declare war or to reserve national revenue by royal command. Yet all these powers, and more, were regarded as inalienable rights by monarchs of past centuries. In the mists of antiquity kings could demand obedience by force and preside over councils in which their word could silence all dissent: now the monarch rules only by the will of the people and to do their will.

At present there are only ten reigning royal families in Europe, in seven kingdoms, a pocket-sized Grand Duchy and two tiny principalities. Defeat in war, internal revolution and majority consensus have swept away the myriad emperors and kings, princes and dukes who held sway over millions of lives only a century ago. Yet at no time since the mid-seventeenth century has the British monarchy been in any real danger of falling. Several times the monarch himself has come under attack—most recently when national outcry against his marriage plans made King Edward VIII feel in conscience bound to abdicate—but there has been no concerted attempt to discard the institution of monarchy in Britain. Presumably it would be possible to force a 'bad' king to give up his throne: were the future Charles III to prove a modern Charles I, demanding vast personal power in government, or a latter-day Charles II, scandalizing his subjects with his blatant *amours*, he might be forced to abdicate. Yet this is a possibility as hard to envisage as that of the permanent deposition of the royal dynasty. Whatever the future of Britain in the European Economic Community in terms of abrogation of national sovereignty, the monarchy is already safeguarded under the terms of the Treaty of Rome. The very fact that such drastic steps seem so unlikely is due largely to the high standard of service rendered to Britain by her royal family in this century. Recent monarchs have served the nation so well, even 'beyond the call of duty', in both war and peace, that it is well-nigh impossible to visualize a time when they might fall short of their present high standard.

A would-be president seeks power, a potential Pope achieves it, but a monarch 'has greatness thrust upon him' by the accident of birth. The British monarch, whatever his intelligence, talents and propensities, is required to undertake duties, both intellectual and practical, diverse and daunting in their scope, which are asked of no other man or woman in the kingdom. Stories of the foibles and failings of British monarchs in a thousand years and more of the nation's history only highlight the country's present good fortune in the royal House of Windsor.

Egbert
802-839

(Ecgbert)

Born ?770–780.
Succeeded as King of Wessex in 802, as overlord (by conquest) of the British of Cornwall and Devon in 815, as King of Kent in 825, as King of the English in 829, and as overlord of Wales in 831.
Married Eadburgh.
Children ÆTHELWULF, Editha, Æthelstan.
Died 839, probably in his sixties, having reigned 37 years.

ﺩﺷﺸﺷﺷﺷﺷﺷﺷﺷﺷﺷﺷﺷ

Egbert was King of the West Saxons at the time when, after the death of Offa, King of Mercia, in 769, Wessex took over the leading position among the three principal kingdoms. Northumbria had been in the ascendant in the seventh century and Mercia in the eighth. The four other rulers in the so-called Hept-archy of England – the kings of East Anglia, Kent, Essex (including the former Middlesex) and Sussex (which, with Kent, had partitioned the old Surrey) – were virtually vassals, and the last three realms were soon part of Wessex. Egbert absorbed the kingdom of Kent in 825, and the territory was occasionally passed to a son or grandson as a means of training in leadership. In 825 Egbert defeated the King of Mercia at the battle of Ellendun (now Wroughton, near Swindon), and his armies fanned out to occupy Mercia. They also demonstrated sufficient military presence on the northern border for Northumbria to pay particular attention to Egbert's political aims in that direction.

All this activity was comparatively minor. There was no great military tyrant crushing the spirit of a helpless nation. But Egbert's supremacy, opera-ted from Wessex, was sufficient for him to take the ancient title of *Bretwalda*, ruler of Britain. This was a mystical, rather than a practical title. No new knees were bent in direct homage and no extra taxes were yielded, yet it is evident that even the kings of Scotland took some notice of those few Saxon kings whose prestige was great enough for

Right *King Egbert of Wessex, carved in relief at Wells Cathedral.*

Below *A delightful woodcut showing King Egbert receiving homage.*

them to be styled King of Britain. Egbert was the last *Bretwalda*. Militarily he could not justify his title for long, since in order to maintain political peace he gave Mercia a sort of independence in 830. But Egbert remained as overlord of the King of East Anglia, and had the kingdoms of Kent, Essex and Sussex in his family pocket, as the Crown today holds the Duchy of Cornwall. The Cornish, or West Welsh, who constantly threatened the other kingdoms, made an alliance with the Danes and jointly invaded Wessex from the west in 838. Their decisive defeat by Egbert at Hengist Down spelt out the epitaph on Cornish power and independence. As the father and trainer of a royal dynasty in Wessex which was to display the foremost military dash and administrative competence, Egbert laid the foundations on which his descendants on the throne of Wessex became the accepted kings of England.

Æthelwulf
839-858

(Ethelwulf)

Born ?800–810
Succeeded as King of Kent 828, King of Wessex 839.
Elder son of his predecessor Egbert.
Married 1. Osburgh who died 846 (or was perhaps 'put away' to allow a dynastic marriage with a younger bride); 2. Judith, daughter of Charles II, King of France, (Charles the Bald).
Children Æthelstan, ÆTHELBALD, ÆTHELBERT, ÆTHELRED, ÆLFRED, Æthelswyth, all the children of Osburgh.
Died 858, probably in his fifties.

꙳꙳꙳꙳꙳꙳꙳꙳꙳꙳꙳꙳

Upon his succession, Æthelwulf gave the sub-kingdom of Kent to his younger brother Æthelstan. After a vigorous beginning to his reign his health declined and he took his fifth son Alfred to Rome, where he stayed a year. He returned in 856, married Judith of France on the journey, and found his eldest surviving son Æthelbald in revolt. (Æthelstan had died in 850). The administration was shared between father and son until Æthelwulf died two years later.

Æthelbald
858-860

(Ethelbald)

Born ?834.
Succeeded as King of Wessex 858 after sharing power from 856.
Second son of his predecessor Æthelwulf.
Married his stepmother, Judith, his father's widow, who after his speedy death married Baldwin I, Count of Flanders. Their son, Baldwin II, married Ælfthryth, daughter of King Alfred and when William the Conqueror married a descendant of this line, Matilda, daughter of Baldwin V, he secured for his sons a renewed affiliation to the direct royal line of Alfred.
Children none.
Died 860, aged about 26, having been sole ruler of Wessex for two years. Buried at Sherborne.

Above *A unique example of early English regalia, this ring was worn by King Æthelwulf.*

Below *Located in the British Museum this woodcut depicts King Æthelbald, who reigned two years.*

Æthelbert
860-866

(Ethelbert)

Born ?836.
Succeeded as King of Kent 853, King of Wessex 860.
Younger brother of his predecessor Æthelbald.
Marriage none recorded.
Children none recorded.
Died 866, aged about 30, having reigned six years. Buried at Sherborne.

Æthelred I
866-871

(Ethelred)
Known as Saint Ethelred

Born ?840.
Succeeded as King of Wessex (henceforth including Kent, Sussex, Essex) 866.
Younger brother of his predecessor Æthelbert.
Wife not known.
Children Æthelhelm, Æthelwald.
Died 871 aged about 31, of wounds

Above *In this nineteenth century illustration, Saint Augustine preaches before King Æthelbert.*

Right *King Æthelred was faced with the first large-scale invasions of England by the Vikings.*

Below *Struck c 870, this coin is engraved with the name and profile of King Æthelred.*

received during the battle of Merton, having reigned five years. Buried at Wimborne.

❖❖❖❖❖❖❖❖❖❖❖❖❖

By the time that the third of Æthelwulf's sons came to the throne, the Danish invasions of Northumbria, Mercia and East Anglia were a serious threat to the survival of Wessex, and Æthelred was leading his armies over the border into Mercia in order to preserve his kingdom. His second-in-command was his 19-year-old brother Alfred. (Their only known sister, Æthelswyth, was then consort to Burghred, King of Mercia). By 871 the West Saxons had had to retreat into their own territory and, after the punishing battle of Merton in that year, Æthelred died, and Alfred took over the task of ensuring the survival of the Anglo-Saxons.

Æthelred was popularly canonized because of his piety. At the vital battle of Ashdown, though Alfred was being pressed hard, Æthelred was kneeling in his tent hearing Mass, and said he would not stir until the Mass was ended and would not serve man before God.

Alfred
871-899

(Ælfred)
Known as Alfred the Great

Born 849 at Wantage.
Succeeded as King of Wessex 871 at the age of 22. Was declared King of the Saxons and King of the English. Recognized as overlord of Wales 893.
Younger brother of his predecessor Æthelred, being the fifth son of King Æthelwulf and the grandson of King Egbert.
Married in 868 to Ealswyth who survived him and died about 902.
Children Æthelflæd, EADWARD, Æthelgeofu, Ælfthryth, Æthelweard.
Died October 28, 899 aged 50, having reigned 28 years. Buried at Winchester.
Profile a clean-shaven, barrel-chinned, deeply-lined perhaps almost tortured face, neither senile nor conventionally 'wise' or great. He was never called Alfred the Great in his lifetime, and the bearded statue of him in Wantage, Berkshire, has the face of a local Victorian.

Alfred's brother and brother-in-arms, Æthelred, had two surviving children when he died. But it was a time for active, experienced leadership, and they were not even considered as possible successors. It is interesting, however, to see how powerful connections had their advantages even so many years ago. One of the boys, Æthelhelm, became Archbishop of Canterbury and the other, Æthelwald, was King of York and indeed tried to take Alfred's throne after his death. However, their uncle's immediate problem was to beat off the Danes from their assault on Wessex. His

Right This exquisite relic of the ninth century is known as the Alfred Jewel. It is inscribed 'Alfred ordered me to be made'.

Below A romantic portrait by Frank Salisbury (1912) depicts King Alfred at the Royal Exchange.

ultimate achievement, which followed in part from the weakened position of the Mercians and Northumbrians against the Danes, was that when the fragmented English kingdoms collapsed before the foreign assault, Alfred had something to put in its place. And the concept of England as a nation hardened into a reality, for under assault it had developed an identity of its own. Alfred was never crowned King of all England, a title which he has sometimes been given retrospectively. That would have been a presumptuous claim, although he well earned his title King of the Saxons, and did style himself on some of his coins as King of the English. His son and successor, Edward the Elder took the title King of the English, but the realm was limited, and only Alfred's grandson Æthelstan brought in Northumbria.

Alfred, as a warrior-king with an urgent objective, fought nine battles against the Danes in the first year of his reign and won himself a breathing-space. He did not, however, reorganize the defense of

Left *Cast in bronze, King Alfred's statue dominates Winchester.*

Below *Alfred shrewdly forced King Guthrum to be baptized after he had defeated him at Edington.*

Wessex with conspicuous brilliance. Though a mature 22 years of age and a hardened commander, he was a late developer intellectually and a most tortured man psychologically. He was troubled by what are nowadays interpreted as psychosomatic illnesses – afflictions reflecting mental unease – and on his wedding day he became mysteriously and incapably sick, a circumstance which modern psychiatrists inevitably seize with glee. Alfred is one of the most fascinating characters in history, and a dramatist of perception could do him the justice of resurrection in the same sense that we now know Sir Thomas More, as 'a man for all seasons'.

A quick impression presents Alfred as a combination of the pious imperial dreamer with the shrewd, long-term-strategy, defensive general. A deeper analysis suggests a man intolerably teased by ambition and humility, with many of his actions being little more than compulsive reactions to the desperate pressure of events. Yet he was also a man able to give practical shape to a serene vision of a new land, advancing under thoughtful laws, adequate security, and a new concept of philosophy and education and culture to meet and appreciate a wider world. Alfred dissolved the insularity of Saxon England in a secular and cultural sense which was far more influential than the formal concept of the universality of the Christian Church. Two youthful sojourns in Rome, where the Pope robed the boy as a consul and sponsored him as a future leader, and a further stay at the court of the King of the Franks, gave him a lasting vision of the spaciousness of the world and the richness of life that arose from contact with it. Yet he was always afflicted by a self-doubt that physically incapacitated him at many crises, and by self-depreciation based on the fact that, like every king's son of his time, he was illiterate – until he conquered this disadvantage towards the end of his life.

For the first seven years of his reign Alfred continued his undistinguished skirmishing with the Danes to try to hold his territory as he had established it during his initial year of vigorous campaigning. In January 878 the Danes made an unconventional winter blitzkreig, and Wessex was completely overrun. But over the next four months Alfred deployed his underground resistance from his base in the Somerset

marshes, and by superb organization welded the men of Somerset, Wiltshire and Hampshire into an army which decisively defeated the Danes in the pitched battle at Edington, Wiltshire. With impressive statesmanship he consolidated this victory. He insisted that the defeated King Guthrum of the Danes should receive baptism into Christianity – probably with less consideration for the welfare of Guthrum's soul than for the well-being of the inhabitants of Danish-occupied Mercia and Northumbria who would undergo less harassment in their native culture if Christianity was a recognized religion. He then drastically conscripted the man-power of Wessex, so that it was efficiently organized as a defense arm and an agricultural workforce, the men taking turns at these complementary duties. He built a chain of fortified towns which would remain as urban strongholds in future invasions, so that Wessex could never be entirely blotted out as it had been in 878. Also he built a navy as a new reserve against the sea-power of the Danes.

In the uneasy, but generally effective, conditions of peace which followed these imaginative defense measures, Alfred established a much-needed judicial system by introducing a new code of laws painstakingly worked out from the best contemporary foreign practice. Then, having learned to read at the age of 38, and having much that he wanted to say to his people in the old English language, Alfred began a cult of broad education which aimed at giving the English a soul, and a sense of corporate history. This resulted in shaping for them an identity which has its hold today. His reign was an example of how a sense of vision could be used by a monarch.

Edward
899-925

(Eadward)
Known as Edward the Elder

Born ?875.
Succeeded 899 as King of Wessex, died as 'King of the English' though he ruled only Wessex and Mercia.
Elder son of predecessor Alfred.
Married 1. Ecgwyn; 2. Æflæd; 3. Eadgifu.

Left *Alfred's eldest son Edward succeeded his father and inherited the benefits of a stable kingdom.*

Below *An unusual view from the back of Winchester Cathedral as it stands today.*

13

Children of Ecgwyn, ÆTHELSTAN, Editha; of Æflæd, Ælfweard, Eadflæd, Eadgifu, Æthelhild, Eadgyth, Ælgifu, Elsfeda, Eadwine and two unnamed daughters; of Eadgifu, EADMUND, EADRED, Elfred, Eadgifu, Eadburgh.
Died 925 having reigned 26 years, aged about 50. Buried at Winchester.

⸎⸎⸎⸎⸎⸎⸎⸎⸎⸎⸎⸎⸎

Edward was the first of three able hereditary rulers from Alfred's stock who gave England 75 years of strength and steady growth, so that its 'national' characteristics were not entirely swamped during the following century of turmoil. His elder sister, Alfred's daughter Æthelflæd, had been joined in dynastic marriage to Æthelred of Mercia, and, using her aid and position as Lady of Mercia, Edward re-conquered the midlands and southeast of England. Edward and his son exploited the institution of dynastic marriage much more thoroughly than his father, and, with 18 children, had more offshoots to graft. Daughters of Edward married kings of France, Burgundy, Provence and York, and one, Eadgyth, married Otto the Great, the Holy Roman Emperor. None of the customary truculent claims to foreign thrones resulted from these unions, but they illustrate the international prestige to which Alfred, Edward, and Edward's son Æthelstan raised England.

Æthelstan
925-940

(Athelstan)

Born 895.
Succeeded as King of the English in 925 at the age of 30, and by his conquests justified that title and his later claim as Emperor of Britain.
Eldest son of his predecessor Edward.
Marriage none recorded.
Children none recorded.
Died October 27, 940 aged 45 having reigned 15 years. Buried at Malmesbury.

⸎⸎⸎⸎⸎⸎⸎⸎⸎⸎⸎⸎⸎

Æthelstan held immediate sway over all England south of the Trent, and moved swiftly to sovereignty over Northumbria, which still included the south of modern Scotland. With three Welsh princes and an impressive tally of Danish earls supporting him, he later moved to the farther north for an invasion of Scotland proper. Subsequently, in the crucial battle of Brunanburh in 937, he defeated a retaliatory invasion by the kings of Scotland and Strathclyde, driving south in alliance with an Irish general. Æthelstan's brother and successor, Edmund, was his second-in-command, and two of his nephews died in the battle.

Æthelstan was an important international personality and, as has been mentioned, five of his sisters married European monarchs. He acquired great wealth, which he largely used to forward

Above A *frontispiece of an old manuscript depicts Æthelstan, Edward's eldest son presenting a bible to Saint Cuthbert.*

a cultural and religious revival, and in pursuit of these interests he acquired a mammoth collection of jewels and contemporary art, and of holy relics. When he died he was buried in his own monastery of Malmesbury Abbey, to which he bequeathed a part of the True Cross and the Crown of Thorns. He enlarged the conception of monarchy within Britain – he was the first English king to be portrayed on coins and in painting wearing a crown – and he styled himself Emperor of the English and Ruler of all Britain.

Edmund I
940-946

(Eadmund)
Called Edmund the Elder

Born ?922.
Succeeded as King of the English in 940 aged about 18. (This makes him a general at Brunanburh at the age of 15, which is not totally impossible).
Eldest surviving brother (by a different mother) of his predecessor Æthelstan.
Married 1. Ælgifu, who died 944; 2. Æthelflæd.
Children of Ælgifu, EDWY, EDGAR.
Died May 26, 946, assassinated for non-political motives, at Pucklechurch, Gloucester, aged about 24 having reigned six years.
Buried at Glastonbury.

༒༒༒༒༒༒༒༒༒༒༒༒

Edmund began his career of state as a very young commanding general, some 27 years junior to his brother, King Æthelstan. His short reign was ended during an affray in his hall when he was stabbed by a robber whom he had previously banished.

Eadred
946-955

(Edred)

Born ?930.
Succeeded as King of the English 946 aged about 16.
Eldest surviving brother of his predecessor Edmund.
Marriage none recorded.
Children none recorded.
Died November 23, 955 at Frome aged about 25 having reigned nine years. Buried at Winchester.

༒༒༒༒༒༒༒༒༒༒༒༒

Eadred was almost completely pre-occupied during his reign with the retention of Northumbria, which, after swearing allegiance to him after his accession, swiftly transferred allegiance to Eric (Bloodaxe) of Norway. The issue was decided only in 954 when Eric was killed in battle.

Above King Edmund was assassinated by Leolf the Robber while celebrating the feast of Augustine.

Edwy
955-959

(Eadwig)
Known as Edwy the Fair

Born ?941.
Succeeded as King of the English 955 at age about 14.
Elder nephew of his predecessor Eadred and elder son of King Edmund I.
Married Ælgifu.
Children none recorded.
Died 959 aged about 18 having reigned four years. Buried at Winchester.

༒༒༒༒༒༒༒༒༒༒༒༒

Edwy, a generally sickly youth, profited by the vigour of his late uncle, so that at his coronation as King of the English he received the submission of the Northumbrians, the Danes, the Welsh and the Scots. But the weakness of his government might well have resulted in the break-up of England had he survived. His younger brother, Edgar, was already challenging him when he died.

Edgar
959-975

(Eadgar)
Known as Edgar the Peaceful, Edgar the Great.

Born ? 943.
Succeeded as King of the English in 959 at the age of about 16, having already been proclaimed King of Mercia in 957.
Younger brother of predecessor Edwy and younger son of King Edmund I.
Married 1. Æthelflæd; 2. Wulfryth; 3. Ælfthryth.
Children of Æthelflæd, EDWARD; of Wulfryth, Eadgyth; of Ælfthryth (Elfrida), Eadmund, ÆTHELRED.
Died July 8, 975 aged about 32 having reigned 16 years. Buried at Glastonbury.

꧁꧂꧁꧂꧁꧂꧁꧂꧁꧂꧁꧂꧁꧂

Young Edgar had been in rebellion against his brother and had taken over Mercia at the age of 14, two years before he officially occupied the English throne. This was an age when some young men could work off their frustration in satisfyingly positive ways. Edgar was also said to have abducted his second wife from a nunnery and only to have married her after she had served a term as his mistress. Making some recompense for this affront to the Church, he gave his royal backing to a notable monastic revival in England – he himself founded forty religious houses – which was important for its cultural overtones. Scholarship and architecture owed much to the new institutions for their blossoming at this period.

Edgar was fortunate in having the energetic advice of no less than three English saints who were living at the time. They were Dunstan, Archbishop of Canterbury, Oswald, Archbishop of York, and Æthelwold, Bishop of Winchester, who were all later canonized – a fact which in itself pays a remarkable tribute to the prestige of Edgar's reign. Edgar was the last of the strong line of Saxon kings fathered by Alfred, who broadened Alfred's laws and propa-

Above *King Edgar.*

Below *Edgar being rowed on the Dee by the Welsh and Scottish kings.*

gated Alfred's culture. Territorially he extended the sphere of influence of the English throne, hastened the integration of the Danes with the English, and stage-managed the publicized recognition of English majesty. The last was notably achieved at a deliberately delayed coronation service at Bath at Whitsuntide 973, 14 years after Edgar's accession, where the king was solemnly anointed and crowned to receive the blessing of the future Saints. In the same year he received the homage of seven Welsh and Scottish kings, in the picturesque public-relations function (or invented non-event) when they were said to have rowed him on the Dee at Chester.

St Æthelwold and St Dunstan were by this time proclaiming Edgar as 'King of the English and of the other people living within Britain'. The combination of the activities of an able young king with three strong-minded prelates who wanted to exalt the office of king for what they saw as the advantage of the Church was very powerful. It contributed towards the emasculation of a vigorous and meddling aristocracy and did much (through ecclesiastical propaganda) to advance the philosophy of the *divine right* of approved kings, who were the channel of all God's blessings except the Holy Mass. It was an English doctrine which was to bear long-term rather than immediate fruit – but it was in writing, which could be quoted later.

Above *After his assassination in his early teens Edward was hastily canonized and became known as Edward the Martyr. This illustration shows both his death, and his canonized state.*

Edward
975-978

(Eadward)
Known as Edward the Martyr

Born ? 963.
Succeeded as King of the English in 975 aged about 12.
Eldest son of his predecessor Edgar.
Died March 18, 978, assassinated at Corfe Castle, aged about 15 having reigned three years. Buried at Wareham, later at Shaftesbury.

※※※※※※※※※※※※※※

Edward, Edgar's eldest son, was entering his teens when his father died, and he had a party backing his claim to the

Left *Edward was the eldest son of Edgar, and his succession was disputed by a party backing his young brother Æthelred.*

throne, formed in opposition to the rival party backing Æthelred. Edward was the son of Edgar's first wife, Æthelred the son of the third wife. (The nun Wulfryth bore a daughter who became an abbess). Æthelred was about seven years old and cannot be considered a politically responsible person at the time. So he must be acquitted of any moral guilt for his brother's murder, which occurred soon enough. In 978 young Edward rode to visit Æthelred at Corfe in Dorset. Æthelred's retainers crowded round him in a mock welcome and stabbed him. The body was swiftly buried at Wareham. But a year later the Ealdorman (chief noble) of Mercia – the title is a reminder that Mercia accepted the dynastically West Saxon King of the English without any dispute involving a Mercian pretender – dug up the corpse and had it reinterred in the royal mausoleum at Shaftesbury. There were inspired whispers that the king's body had not been corrupted by decay, though, paradoxically, some parts of the skeleton were piously filched as holy relics. The new king, the unfortunate Æthelred, was ready enough to compound some of his guilt-by-implication in a brother's murder by acknowledging him as a Saint, (canonization being then a less rigorously filtered process), and the dead youth became King Edward the Martyr.

Æthelred II
978-1013,
1014-1016

(Ethelred)
Known as Ethelred the Unready

Born ? 968.
Succeeded as King of the English in 978 aged about 10.
Younger brother of his murdered predecessor Edward, and younger son of King Edgar.
Married 1. Ælfgifu of Mercia; 2. Emma of Normandy.
Children of Ælfgifu, Æthelstan, Ecgbert, EADMUND, Eadred, Eadwig, Eadgar, Wulfhild, Eadgyth, Ælfgifu and two other daughters; of Emma, EDWARD, Alfred, Goda.

Above *Corfe castle, site of Edward's assassination.*

Below left *A coin with Æthelred's profile.*

Below right *A silver disc belonging to Æthelred's wife Emma.*

Died in London April 23, 1016 aged 48 having reigned 37 years. Buried in St Paul's Cathedral.

ﾟ･ﾟ･ﾟ･ﾟ･ﾟ･ﾟ･ﾟ･ﾟ･ﾟ

Æthelred was brought to the throne at the age of ten by the crude hatchet-men who had killed his elder brother. All through his life this hapless king was to be a pawn in the power-game, and in view of his weak position he showed a certain political shrewdness and considerable powers of survival. His nickname Æthelred Unræd, which has no reference to being 'unready' is best understood as a skit on his name. This, spelt in its older Saxon form, is Æthelræd, meaning 'noble policy'. The adjective Unræd means 'with no reputable policy', and carries a hint of dirty business, which could refer to the murder of King Edward. The nickname is therefore not affectionately tolerant, but a positive denigration, and has much more affinity with double dealing than simple weakness.

Æthelred's permanent disadvantage was that he could not count on reliable support from his political generals at a time when national unity and forceful military leadership was the only combination which could have saved England from the increasingly menacing attacks of the ambitious Danes. For many years Æthelred, using much the same sincere reasoning which is still advanced to justify the Munich capitulation of 1938, bought off the Danes with inflationary payments of protection money. But:
'If once you have paid him the Dane-geld,
    You never get rid of the Dane',
and in 1009 Sweyn, King of the Danes, who had been actively nibbling away at Æthelred's territory, produced his 'last territorial demand', which was nothing less than England itself. By 1013 he had over-run the country, and Æthelred fled to Normandy, where his second wife Emma had already retreated to join her brother Richard the Good, Duke of Normandy, father of Robert the Devil, father of William the Bastard.

ETHELRED II

KINGS of ENGLAND

·**Right** *King Æthelred.*

Sweyn
1013-1014

(Svegn)
Known as Forkbeard

Born ? 965.
Succeeded as King of Denmark in 986, as King of Norway in 995, as *de facto* King of England (Æthelred having fled abroad) in the winter of 1013 aged about 48.
Married 1. Gunhilda who died 992; 2. Sigrid who died 995.
Children all of Gunhilda, Gytha, Harald, CNUT, Thyra, Estrith.
Died at Gainsborough February 3, 1014, from a fall from his horse, aged 48, having reigned little more than a month. Buried first in London, later in Denmark.

❧❧❧❧❧❧❧❧❧❧❧❧❧

Sweyn had sent his earls to harass England by invasion with increasing attrition from the year 1009. In 1012, after receiving an enormous sum in Dane-geld, the earls murdered Ælfeah, Archbishop of Canterbury (St Alphege). In 1013 Sweyn, commanding his naval forces in person, occupied England. He died after a fall from his horse during an army advance – traditionally struck down in the course of a hallucination that the sainted martyr King Edward, whom he had obsessionally hated, rode towards him in full armour to challenge him in single combat. Sweyn's youngest daughter Estrith possibly married Robert, Duke of Normandy, but she was not the mother of William the Conqueror.

Edmund II
1016

(Eadmund)
Known as Edmund Ironside

Born ? 990.
Succeeded as King of England April 23, 1016 aged about 26.
Eldest surviving son of his predecessor Æthelred II.

Married Ealdgyth.
Children Edward, Edmund.
Died November 30, 1016 in London, probably murdered, at the age of 26 having reigned seven months. Buried at Glastonbury.

❧❧❧❧❧❧❧❧❧❧❧❧❧

After the sudden death of Sweyn of Denmark there were three candidates for the throne. Sweyn's eldest son Cnut had possession of the throne, with command of his late father's forces and with control of the royal treasury, such as it was in an uncertain time of war and lapsed taxes. But Cnut, then aged about 19, decided to defer his claim and he went back to Denmark to consolidate his forces, having first mutilated, with Viking ruthlessness, the English hostages whom his father had taken from London and all the shires. The throne therefore fell by default to its original occupant Æthelred, who had never formally abdicated. But Æthelred's eldest surviving son Edmund, (called Ironside because of his physical strength), disputed his father's capacity to rule with sufficient virility to protect England from the Danes.

This problem was resolved by Æthelred's death in April 1016. However, Cnut had already returned with strong forces in 1015, and a slight majority of the English ealdormen (the nobility of the shires) saw more chance of achieving swift law and order with Cnut as king rather than Edmund. If there had been a full meeting of the English magnates at that time it is probable that Cnut would have obtained a narrow vote of confidence. He did not bother with this formality, but proclaimed himself king and conspired against the lives of Edmund and

Below King Edmund II.

Opposite Cnut with his queen.

others in the Saxon succession. Edmund therefore virtually manipulated his own accession. He summoned in London a meeting of the king-making council, the *Witanagemot*. Only those members who lived near London, or were there at the time on business, were able to attend. Sincerely pursuing their own advantage, this 'Rump of the Witan', the equivalent of powerful money-men of today, named Edmund as king (i.e., they 'elected' him), and immediately the citizens of London acclaimed him. The rival kings began to spar for initial advantages in a military trial of strength which culminated in victory for Cnut at the battle of Ashingdon in October 1016. Next month Edmund died suddenly, reputedly assassinated by being stabbed.

Cnut
1016-1035

(Canute)

Born ?995.

Succeeded as King of Denmark and Norway in 1014, as King of England November 30, 1016, aged about 21.

No relationship to predecessor Edmund save that he married Edmund's stepmother, Æthelred's widow.

Married 1. Ælfgifu of Northampton, whom he did not divorce, but he continued to live with her when in Denmark (where she was acknowledged queen) after he married Emma of Normandy, widow of his predecessor Æthelred.

Children of Ælfigfu ,Svegn, HAROLD; of Emma, HARTHACNUT, Gunhild.

Died at Shaftesbury November 12, 1035 aged 40, having reigned 18 years. Buried at Winchester.

❀❀❀❀❀❀❀❀❀❀❀❀❀

Cnut was a second-generation Christian, and by no means meek or mild. After the murder of Edmund Ironside, which cannot be positively ascribed to him, he disposed of further heirs of the Saxon line by having Edmund's younger brother Eadwig murdered and by sending Edmund's young sons Edward and Edmund into exile in Hungary.

Since he had determined to marry Æthelred's widow Emma, to retain some of the magic of a connection with the previous reigning house (Æthelbald, 858-860, did the same for less obvious reasons) Cnut could hardly murder Edmund's stepbrothers, the sons of Emma, and they were sent to Normandy. One of them, Alfred, was later murdered – not by Cnut – in further skirmishing for the throne in 1036. The survivor, Edward, eventually reigned after Cnut and his two sons, as Edward the Confessor. The long exile in Normandy, which virtually made Edward a Norman, is some explanation of why the line of royal claimants to the throne in England veered away from Scandinavia towards Normandy.

After his initial liquidation and exile of positive claimants to the throne, Cnut went on to conduct a purge of Englishmen in his entourage through half a dozen selected assassinations. He then ostentatiously married Emma, leaving the position of his previous wife

Ælfgifu and her children in considerable legal uncertainty, though that did not prevent one of them succeeding him. From this point on, Cnut settled down to govern England with outstanding efficiency. If ever the argument that the means justify the end was admissable, Cnut seems to have demonstrated that a few shrewd murders coupled with sanctified adultery, all tidily performed before one's 21st birthday, should not for ever bar a man from the reputation of having a heart of gold.

While Cnut lived, there was none of the internal manoeuvring for power which Æthelred had had to balance. However he tolerated potentially dangerous threats from his three extremely powerful *earls* (the new title, of Danish origin, replaced the Saxon *ealdorman*): Siward of Northumbria, Leofric of Mercia, and Godwin of Wessex. Cnut had new ideals concerning kingship. He ruled from strength, or fear, but he strove to incorporate two strong traditions, wider justice based on pragmatic

Above *A beautifully preserved coin at the Ashmolean Museum Oxford depicting Cnut's profile.*

Below *An engraving in the nineteenth century romantic manner depicting the legend that Cnut could halt the waves.*

law-making and aimed at righting perceived wrongs, in the spirit of the great Alfred and Edgar; and the application of Christian principles to monarchy, even if the conception of monarchy as a trust from God was interpreted in a somewhat naive and authoritarian manner by this *parvenu* Christian.

As a ruler not only of England, but of Denmark and Norway and, for a time, a part of Sweden, Cnut's prestige and temporal power within Europe – which he toured on a long state visit ending in Rome – was second only to the Holy Roman Emperor's. The story that such a capable king could be fooled by flattering courtiers to sit by the sea and order the retreat of the incoming tide must be dismissed as a myth of propaganda and popular folklore.

Harold I
1035-1040

Known as Harold Harefoot

Born 1017.
Succeeded as regent, later King of England November 12, 1035 at the age of 18.
Son of his predecessor Cnut through Cnut's first wife Ælfgifu.
Marriage none recorded.
Children none recorded.
Died at Oxford March 17, 1040 aged 23 having reigned five years.
Buried at Westminster, and later in St Clement Danes, London, the body having been disinterred from the Abbey by Harthacnut, thrown into a ditch, and recovered from the Thames by a fisherman.

꧁ꙮꙮꙮꙮꙮꙮꙮꙮꙮꙮꙮ꧂

Cnut's failing was that he could not prevent the resurgence of internal faction after his death. Since, in a nebulous situation of legitimacy, Emma was his official wife in England, his logical heir was their son Harthacnut. Harthacnut, already King of Denmark, was engaged in a power struggle with Magnus, King of Norway, which had established independence. He claimed the English throne, backed by Emma

Left *Harold I, son of Cnut and the Danish Queen Ælgifu was sponsored to the throne by Earl Leofric and his supporters.*

Below *Boar hunting was a favourite pastime of Saxon kings.*

and Earl Godwin, but could not immediately secure it.

Earl Leofric and his political supporters sponsored Harold, the son of Cnut and Ælfgifu. A claim of strong standing lay with Alfred and Edward, the sons of Emma by her first husband King Æthelred. But when Alfred came over from Normandy he was murdered on the orders of Earl Godwin. Harold was accepted, first as regent, then as king.

Harthacnut
1040-1042

(Hardecnut)
Means literally Deadly Cnut

Born 1018.
Succeeded as King of Denmark 1035, as King of England March 17, 1040 aged 22.
Half-brother of his predecessor Harold through their father Cnut, Harold's predecessor.
Marriage none recorded.
Children none recorded.
Died drunk at Lambeth June 8, 1042 aged 24 having reigned two years. Buried at Winchester.

❦❦❦❦❦❦❦❦❦❦❦❦

In a treaty with Magnus, King of Norway, Harthacnut, while King of Denmark, had agreed that if either of them died without an heir the survivor should inherit his rival's dominion. Once Harthacnut was King of England, and Magnus indicated that this land, too, was part of his legacy, Harthacnut changed his mind. He brought out of exile in Normandy King Æthelred's only surviving and un-murdered son, Edward, who was his half-brother, being the son of Emma. Having designated Edward as his heir, Harthacnut collapsed in his cups at a wedding banquet, and died immediately in convulsions.

Above right *A finely engraved portrait of Harthacnut, who disputed the throne with Magnus of Norway.*

Below right *The great seal of King Edward the Confessor showing him seated on the throne.*

HARDICANUTE

Opposite above *Edward the Confessor, king and saint, heals a leper outside Westminster Abbey.*

Opposite below *A relief carving of Edward the Confessor at Westminster Abbey which he founded.*

Edward
1042-1066

Known (later) as Saint Edward the Confessor

Born ? 1004.
Succeeded as King of England June 8, 1042 aged about 38.
Half-brother to his predecessor Harthacnut through their mother Emma. Son of King Æthelred II, his fifth predecessor.
Married Eadgyth (Edith) daughter of Earl Godwin of Wessex and Kent.
Children none.
Died at Westminster January 5, 1066 aged 62 having reigned 24 years. Buried at Westminster.
Profile Even in middle age, when he ascended the throne, Edward resembled a sort of Saxon Father Christmas, with pale yellow hair and beard (not white) and a notably pink complexion. He was a courtly, comfort-loving, man and should not be thought of as the gaunt ascetic with the white wizard's beard – the image which was later wished on him.

༶༺༒༺༒༺༒༺༒༺༒༺༒༺༒༺༒

Edward, in the direct hereditary line of Alfred, Edgar and Æthelred, had been brought up as a Young Pretender, a prince in exile from the age of 12 who had no serious expectations of the English throne. He was an idle, sporting, cultured aristocrat who only in later years turned to the piety with which he is now credited. His culture, and indeed his language, was Norman-French, which is why Westminster Abbey was built (before the Conquest) in the Norman style. From the beginning of his reign Edward had to submit to the arrogance of his father-in-law, Earl Godwin, knowing that Godwin had murdered his brother Alfred. But any idea Godwin may have had that a grandson of his would inherit the throne collapsed when Eadgyth failed to bear children. In the later holy cult of Edward as Confessor (Confessor is a rank in the progression towards sainthood and designates a person who was persecuted for his faith but not martyred), the circumstance of Eadgyth's sterility was advanced as a proof of Edward's

25

chastity, but there is no evidence of this at all.

In 1051, when it was rumoured that Godwin might seek to have a son of his, rather than a grandson, succeed to Edward's throne – a project which actually came to fruition with the accession of Eadgyth's brother, Harold Godwinson – Edward unexpectedly banished Queen Eadgyth, exiled Godwin, and proclaimed his natural cousin William of Normandy as his heir. The stroke was premature. It was soon reversed, and William's designation to the succession was virtually cancelled.

Godwin died, and Edward adopted a working friendship with Harold Godwinson, who was conveniently relieving him of many of his duties. But, still anxious over the succession, Edward recalled from Hungary Edward the Exile, son of King Edmund Ironside, whom Cnut had banished 40 years previously. But Edward the Exile died

in suspicious circumstances before the interview with his uncle could take place. His young son Edgar Ætheling had a strong hereditary claim to the throne on the death of Edward the Confessor, whose master-work of Westminster Abbey was dedicated a week before he died, and whose canonization was effected a century later.

Harold II
1066

Known as Godwinson

Born ? 1022.
Succeeded as King of England January 5, 1066 aged about 44.
Brother-in-law to his predecessor Edward.
Married 1. Eadgyth Swan-neck, 2.

Above *The Bayeux Tapestry, one of the most famous in the world, is 213ft long and 20in wide. It represents the sequence of events in the Norman conquest of England in 72 scenes. Seven of them are shown here.*
Reading from left to right: *in 1064, Harold visits William with a message from Edward the Confessor that William is to succeed him. Then Edward dies, having*

first nominated Harold as his successor. His body is taken to Westminster Abbey. The next panel shows William preparing for war, having heard the news that Harold has been crowned king. The next panel shows him setting sail for England with men and horses on board, then, in the following panel, landing at Pevensey. In the meantime Harold had been occupied fighting in the north, and did not hear of William's landing until four days later, when he force marched his troops south to meet William. The next panel shows a scene from the Battle of Hastings in which the mounted Normans have a decisive advantage over the English defenders who are already exhausted. In the final scene, Harold is seen plucking the fatal arrow from his eye.

The tapestry was commissioned by Bishop Odo of Bayeux, and was probably made in England within 20 years of the Conquest. It clearly shows the difference in the types of weapons used. William had the monopoly of well-equipped archers, and fully trained cavalry, while the English defenders relied on the battle axe.

Ealdgyth, widow of Gruffydd; ap Llywelyn.

Children of Eadgyth, Godwine, Eadmund, Magnus, Ulf, Gytha, Gunhild; of Ealdgyth, Harold.

Died in battle at Hastings October 14, 1066 aged 44 having reigned ten months. Buried at Pevensey, later in Waltham Abbey.

ᘛᖇᘚᖇᘚᖇᘚᖇᘚᖇᘚᖇᘚᖇᘚᖇᘚ

Harold Godwinson, son and successor to the ambitious Godwin, Earl of Wessex, and brother of Edward's widowed queen, had been commander-in-chief of the forces and 'under-king' – in practice, regent – during Edward's last years. The *Witanagemot* did not hesitate to by-pass the claim of the 15-year-old Edgar Ætheling and ignore William of Normandy by promptly proclaiming Harold as king. And Harold underlined the urgency by having himself crowned in Westminster Abbey on the day following Edward's death. He was a man of great vigour, confidence (perhaps over-confidence) and ex-

perience; and one of the most intriguing of all theories is the reconstruction of how England would have developed if – as so easily might have been the case – he had not died at Hastings and lost the battle. Harold's marriage, two years previously, to the widow of Gruffydd ap Llywelyn, Ruler of All Wales, was a rare dynastic connection between the English and the British, though Ealdgyth was not born a Celt.

Harold's immediate task on his accession was to defend England from the consequences of two anticipated invasions, from Norway and Normandy – he had not the resources to meet these problems by destroying invasion forces before they sailed or landed. Harold Hardrada, King of Norway, had inherited the pretensions of his predecessor Magnus to the throne of England, and was supported by Harold Godwinson's dissident brother Tostig, exiled Earl of Northumbria. After months of suspense the Norwegians invaded first. King Harold brushed them out of English history by defeating

them at Stamford Bridge in Yorkshire, where both Hardrada and Tostig were killed, on September 25, 1066. While celebrating the victory at York, Harold learned that William of Normandy had landed in Sussex. He force-marched south and met the enemy forces, who had had a fortnight to consolidate their order of battle, on the ridge above Hastings where Battle Abbey now stands. Through the long day of October 14, the fateful struggle proceeded. It was a story-book battle, hard-fought, with changing fortunes, and even included sensational single combat: King Harold and his two brothers against Duke William and his two half-brothers. At sunset Harold, who had seen his brothers die but still retained a reasonable chance of victory, was the target of a concentrated 'blunderbuss' discharge of arrows. He collapsed with a head wound and was immediately pounced upon and killed.

Below *Harold's body is found.*

28

William I
1066-1087

Known as William the Bastard, and, later, the Conqueror

Born 1027.

Succeeded as Duke of Normandy 1035 aged eight, crowned as King of England December 25, 1066 at the age of 39.

No relation to his predecessor Harold. Second cousin to King Edward the Confessor, William's father being the nephew of Emma, mother of Edward, (i.e. Edward's mother was William's great-aunt).

Married Matilda of Flanders, a descendant of King Alfred through his daughter Ælfthryth, who married Baldwin II, Count of Flanders.

Children Robert, Richard, Cecily, WILLIAM, Adeliza, Constance, Adela, Agatha, Matilda, HENRY.

Died in action against the French, from a riding mishap which ruptured intestines already weakened by dysentery, at Rouen on September 6, 1087, aged 60, having reigned 21 years. Buried at Caen.

Profile In 1085, when the *Domesday Book* was planned, he was tallish, thick, regal, stern, and very imposing in spite of a notably protuberant belly and a balding head.

❖❖❖❖❖❖❖❖❖❖❖❖❖❖

When Harold fell at Hastings, William did not immediately succeed as king. The English had not surrendered, and their leaders considered proclaiming young Edgar Ætheling. But William conducted a vengeful war of attrition, laying waste the shires round London. Under pressure the generals capitulated, and the *Witanagemot*, in the last official function of this historic institution,

Above left *A map of England and France at the time of the Conquest, showing Harold's battles in the north.*

Above right *After the Conquest William rewarded the Norman barons with land. Here he is shown bestowing land on his nephew, the Earl of Brittany.*

accepted William and attended his coronation in Westminster Abbey on Christmas Day 1066.

William was the only son of the Duke of Normandy, Robert the Devil, the offspring of an intense and undying love-affair with Herleva (Herlève), the daughter of a burgher of Falaise known as William the Tanner. The conventions of the time forbade a marriage between Robert and Herleva, since the marriages of nobility were reserved for political purposes – such as a claim on territory

Above *The famous* Domesday Book, *compiled for William I.*

Left *Falaise castle, France, birthplace of William the Conqueror.*

Right *Battle Abbey commemorates the Norman victory at Hastings.*

of the bride's father or some other substantial dowry – rather than for romantic reasons. Nevertheless, Robert seems to have remained, through his short life, monumentally faithful to Herleva although she in her turn had to be married off for the usual materialist reasons to a Norman baron. From this marriage she had two sons, Robert and Odo, William's half-brothers who supported him in the spectacular single combat at Hastings. Odo, Bishop of Bayeaux, was an old-style bishop, a fighting and administrative feudal lord rather than a devout cleric; his priceless legacy to history was the commissioning of the Bayeux Tapestry.

William's father died on a pilgrimage to Jerusalem in 1035. Yet the boy, then aged eight, managed, as Robert's only child, however irregular his birth, to find enough support to retain the Dukedom of Normandy against continuous campaigns of intrigue, assassination and foreign invasion, particularly by the King of France. Through 20 turbulent years he developed his generalship, his political skill, and a genuine interest in the reform of the Church.

The invasion of England was a complete success. It was a carefully planned campaign, not only on the part of William himself but also by many who supported him. Barons and knights from Flanders and Brittany, who owed William no feudal service, made a shrewd calculation of his chances of victory and invested in the prospect of his success by joining his army and – what was absolutely essential – contributing the capital necessary to build a fleet of invasion barges. Their judgement proved sound, and they collected their dividends. In this instance the profit was colossal. It amounted eventually to no less than three-quarters of the whole territory of England, shared out piecemeal among about 5000 adventurers – either warriors of ecclesiastics – with the other quarter of the land being retained · by William. The property-owning democracy (which did exist among English freemen to a certain extent) and the old, almost independent aristocracy of the Saxon-Danish landowners were entirely expropriated.

William first used the tremendous wastage of the English nobility at Hastings to transfer the land once held by the defeated owners to his Norman followers and speculators from Flanders

and Brittany. He then extended expropriation to cover the land of all who had once acknowledged Harold as king. He completed the transfer by using every one of the many subsequent rebellions against the Conquest as an occasion for the take-over of property. He was able to crush every rebellion, even when the Welsh and fresh contingents of Danes burst in to challenge him, because of the fragmentation which England had suffered in the preceding century, with the loss of any corporate and united resolution to survive. The revolts were desperate, but uncoordinated and sporadic, rather than organized. William settled them one by one, like a terrier killing rats.

This stern conqueror seized the opportunity of the later rebellions to apply unprecedented sanctions of massacre and devastation, stabilizing his domination through terror. In old Mercia and Northumbria his bloody suppression depopulated whole areas, so that hundreds of gutted villages were still only empty names by the time that his catalogue of property was compiled in the *Domesday Book*. In many areas these smoking graveyards were replaced by the stone Norman castles – which were not the havens of the fortified towns which Alfred had instituted, but war-centres deliberately constructed as bases of aggression to ensure the perpetual domination of the invaders. (The Tower of London was built high, *outside* the city walls). This was the most rigorous, swift and revolutionary military occupation in history.

England passed through the fire to be forged into a nation, helplessly subject but more united through subjection than it had ever been before. Yet the land was still individual. The feudal system, based on the tenancy of multiple small parcels of land rather than on European-style provinces or Saxon-Danish earldoms, had an entirely different character from elsewhere, and was much more autocratically dominated by the king. There was still, however, an English heritage. William had sworn to observe the old Saxon laws, and he kept this promise because it was convenient to him. He set up specifically ecclesiastical courts for spiritual and matrimonial matters, banishing the local bishop from the criminal and civil business of the shire court. He thus built up the authority of the shire court, which administered the King's Justice within the king's own administrative unit (the shire, or county) – effectively reducing any independent despotism on the part of the largest land-owner in that county. It was a countermeasure of regal power to check the frequently rebellious aspirations of the immigrant barons, who had cheerfully accepted a vested interest in the new *status quo* with William's extensive grants of land – and realized too late that conditions were not going to be as favourable for them as they would have been under the feudalism of the continental mainland. At the same time, William introduced a clerical bureaucracy (i.e., a civil service in priestly orders) answerable to him and not to the Church, to shape the new establishment.

William the Conqueror was a king of iron, ruthlessly crushing opposition to his policies and his pleasures – which centred on hunting, not women – by violence and mutilation. Strangely, he relied on blinding and maiming rather than hanging, so it has therefore been claimed that capital punishment for crime was non-existent during his reign – a statement which must surely be received with cynicism when one

considers the scores of thousands of noncombatants who were slain by his orders during his 'pacification'. William died as a man of war, defending his Normandy inheritance from the attacks of the King of France. He had become, through the chances of war, England's first total conqueror, and his successors used their interest in his original inheritance to shape England's first imperialism. This eventually led to the acquisition of the Angevin Empire.

Above *A map showing the movements of Harold and William in 1066. Harold was occupied with Norwegian invaders, and returned south when he heard of William's landing at Pevensey.*

Right *An equestrian statue of William at Falaise, his birthplace.*

William II
1087-1100

Known as William Rufus

Born ? 1056.
Succeeded as King of England September 6, 1087 aged about 31.
Second surviving son of his predecessor William.
Marriage none recorded.
Children none recorded.
Died August 2, 1100 from an arrow wound received in mysterious circumstances in the New Forest, aged about 44, having reigned 13 years. Buried in Winchester Cathedral.
Profile Penetrating eyes, medium height, thick build, red face, a lively man, wilfully unconventional in his deliberate blasphemy and colourful oaths, with which he often began a remark to cover an incipient stammer; extravagant with a particularly flamboyant taste in clothes.

༺ ༒ ༒ ༒ ༒ ༒ ༒ ༒ ༒ ༻

William the Conqueror's eldest son, Robert, had rebelled against his father and had tried to seize Normandy. There was a reconciliation, though the disloyalty grieved William even on his deathbed. The Conqueror barred Robert from succession to the English throne, but bequeathed Normandy to him. The next son, Richard, had died seven years earlier – ominously, in a hunting accident in the New Forest – and the Conqueror designated his next son, William, to sovereignty over England. There was a fourth son, Henry, born after a succession of five daughters, and born after the Conqueror was crowned as King of England – 'born in the purple' as the phrase was used. Henry was convinced that this fact gave him a stronger claim to immediate accession than any of his elder brothers, and this conviction of his has been used to shed a sinister light on the events of his actual succession.

William Rufus has been generally described as avaricious, an oppressor of the Church, and in his private life totally immoral. His avarice, which governed his attitude to the Church, may in part be explained by his realization that his father, the Conqueror, had been too generous in his gifts of English land and had not reserved sufficient revenue for the extensive military operations which were still necessary to define and hold the borders of England. Admittedly, he had a passion for personal pleasure and adornment, but he had to spend much more on a series of campaigns against the Scots and the Welsh – as a result of which he built Carlisle Castle and a chain of forts along the Welsh marches – as well as accepting the necessity of facing up to fairly continuous threats from his brother Robert of Normandy. One of the means by which he raised his money was by not filling vacancies in abbeys and bishoprics, and letting the revenues accrue to his treasury.

In such circumstances, since it was the monks who were at that time the historians of England, it is understandable that he did not get favourable notices. The gossip extended to his private life. The fact that he did not marry is nowadays somewhat facilely interpreted as showing that he was homosexual. This is not impossible, but what evidence there is, though it is vague, is to the contrary. His obscure death from an arrow-wound received in the New Forest has caused much later

Left *An artist's impression of the death of Rufus, with his assassin fleeing the scene of the crime.*

speculation, including a modern theory that it was the culmination of a ritual of ancient, pre-Christian, magic using the old formula of 'The King must die'. Walter Tyrell, the man said to have shot him by accident, always denied that he was there at all. A recent theory that the act was murder at the instigation of Henry, who believed he had been lawful king since 1087, has the circumstantial backing that Henry was a member of the fatal hunting party and, as soon as he heard of his brother's death, he rode post-haste to Winchester to commandeer the royal treasury. He took it immediately to London, while bearers more slowly brought Rufus's body to the cathedral. It was buried with little ceremony, beneath the flagstones under the tower, and in the following year the tower fell down. But even the propagandist monk who recorded this could not ascribe the fact to William's godlessness. 'It would have fallen down in any case', he conceded, 'because it was so badly built'.

Henry I
1100-1135

Known as Henry Beauclerk because he was the first king since Alfred who could read fluently.
Known also as the Lion of Justice.

Born 1068.
Succeeded as King of England August 2, 1100 aged 32, as *de facto* Duke of Normandy 1106.
Younger brother of his predecessor William, and fourth son of William the Conqueror.
Married 1. On his accession, Matilda (Eadgyth) daughter of King Malcolm III of Scotland and his queen, (Saint) Margaret, who was a sister of Edgar Ætheling and grand-daughter of Edmund Ironside; died 1118; 2. Adela of Brabant and Louvain, in 1120.
Children all of Matilda: a son who died young; William who was drowned in the wreck of the White Ship, 1120; and Matilda (Maud) who after a short-lived

marriage to the Emperor Henry V married Geoffrey, Count of Anjou (the Angevin, nicknamed Plantagenet).

Mistresses the most notable of many is Nesta, daughter of Rhys ap Tewdr (Tudor), ruling prince of South Wales.

Bastards Henry generously acknowledged 20 illegitimate children, which is presumed to be only a selection of his offspring. The most notable is the learned Robert, Earl of Gloucester, whom he dearly loved and who voluntarily renounced the disputed succession on the ground of his illegitimacy, notwithstanding the success of his grandfather, the Conqueror.

Died at Lyons-la-Forêt, Normandy, on December 1, 1135, of dysentery after over-eating lampreys, an uncharacteristic happening since he was generally abstemious and lampreys (vertebrates looking like eels, yet strictly not fishes) were his only indulgence. He was aged 67 and had reigned 35 years. Buried at Reading Abbey.

Profile Dark hair, like all his family, but with the tendency to a receding hairline masked by combing it into a Roman fringe over his forehead; a thick-set figure accentuated by the family paunch.

ଏଢ଼ଏଢ଼ଏଢ଼ଏଢ଼ଏଢ଼ଏଢ଼ଏଢ଼

Henry was credited by his most flattering chronicler with the vices of avarice, cruelty and lust. In this respect, therefore, he does not seem to have differed from his brother Rufus, yet most contemporary comparisons of the two appear to agree that Henry was more ruthless in his extortion of money and more barbaric in his savagery against the subject – particularly the conspirator, the criminal or the tax-dodger. But there was a correspondingly harder streak in his efficiency of government, particularly in the spheres of defense, finance and justice.

Henry had, almost literally, seized the crown – staging a coronation service three days after Rufus's death – before his elder brother Robert, who had many supporters in England, completed the last lap of his return from a crusade. Henry immediately negotiated marriage with Matilda of Scotland, which not only pumped back the blood of Alfred into his heirs but offered some promise of security on his northern border. The King of the Scots

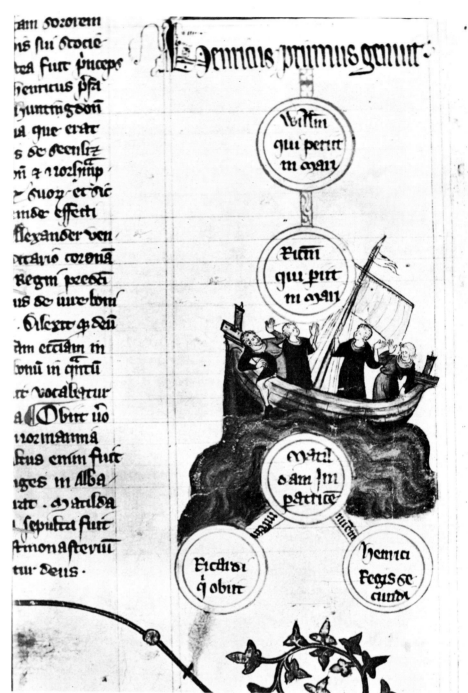

Above *The wreck of the White Ship in which Prince William son of King Henry I was drowned.*

Left and **opposite above** *Two likenesses of Henry I who, as part of the price of his accession had to offer the people a Charter of Liberties.*

had done homage to him on his accession and later recognized his daughter. His brother Robert of Normandy did not give up his ambitions for England, and kept Henry ruefully aware that, in the days of Rufus, Henry and Robert had plotted jointly to secure the throne, ostensibly for Robert. The climax came when Henry defeated Robert in battle at Tinchebrai in 1106, and imprisoned him for life (a further 28 years) in Cardiff Castle, taking over Normandy virtually from that date. Henry then had space and time to improve affairs at home.

Part of the price of his accession had been to offer the people of England a *Charter of Liberties* which, as far as individual freedoms went, was a scrap of paper with the only merit that it could be thrust at King John a century later as a significant archive to demonstrate the virtues of the good old days. Administratively, however, Henry's reorganization of the judiciary and of finance (he appointed the first Chancellor of the Exchequer) did introduce new liberties of law and order, paid for by heavy taxes imposed impartially on Normans and Saxons. Moreover, by forcing a compromise with the Pope, whereby the king retained the baronial (not spiritual) homage of bishops, and had positive influence in appointing them, Henry preserved certain liberties of pride and conscience for his peasants as well as his peers, and undoubtedly prevented the land from becoming priest ridden.

With the death of Henry's heir in 1120 – his wife Matilda having died two years previously – Henry was once more excessively worried about the succession. He married again, but produced no legitimate heir. He required his barons to swear allegiance to his daughter Matilda 'The Empress', widow of Emperor Henry of Germany and wife of Count Geoffrey of Anjou. Yet, confusing the issue even if he was keeping his options open, he cultivated his favourite nephew, Stephen, and nurtured him as a possible heir. He gave him vast estates in Lancashire and Normandy, and married him back into the ancient royal Saxon bloodstock, to a Saxon-Scot, Matilda of Boulogne who also owned very extensive property in what was then known as Flanders. The marriage brings a triple confusion of names. Stephen married Matilda, niece of Henry's first wife Matilda (or Eadgyth, or Edith) of Scotland. Henry I and Matilda of Scotland had a daughter, the Empress Matilda, who is historically the most important of the three and challenged Stephen in the next reign. All the Matildas were descended from Alfred the Great. Henry had a longer life and a longer reign than any of his predecessors, but, later, three kings to a century was quite an ordinary score. In religion he was conformist-pious, and he built Reading Abbey as a Benedictine house to receive his corpse.

Stephen
1135-1154

Born 1097.

Succeeded as King of England (not Duke of Normandy) December 1, 1135 aged about 38.

Nephew of his predecessor Henry, being third son (and not eldest surviving son) of Adela, daughter of William the Conqueror.

Married Matilda of Boulogne, granddaughter of Malcolm III of Scotland.

Children Baldwin, Matilda, Eustace Count of Boulogne (died 1153), Mary, William Count of Boulogne (died 1160).

Died of dysentery, intestinal obstruction and haemorrhoids at Canterbury on October 25, 1154 aged about 57, having reigned 19 years. Buried at Faversham Abbey.

༺༝༝༝༝༝༝༝༝༝༝༝༺

Stephen lunged for the throne on the death of Henry almost as purposefully as Henry had done on the death of Rufus, and he had had himself crowned by Christmas, before the Empress Matilda could rally the many English nobles who supported her claim, or that of her two-year-old son Henry. (Stephen had been the first to swear future allegiance to Matilda when Henry I demanded this of his barons). Stephen's great prop in the early years was his powerful and wealthy younger brother, Henry of Blois, Bishop of Winchester and Abbot of Glastonbury. But Henry I had successfully weakened the power of prelates, so that the authority of the Bishop of Winchester, even as Papal Legate, was not enough to fill the vacuum created by an incompetent king. Stephen failed to measure up to the standards of strength and ruthlessness demanded of a twelfth-century monarch. He reigned, but did not rule. In his weakness he allowed barons and *parvenus* to increase their privileges and military power at the expense of the old royal prerogative – where comparative despotism at least spelt out basic law and order – but not to such an extent that an effective rival sovereignty emerged. The result was anarchy, and misery amid the collapse

country for nine years, during part of which she held Stephen himself a prisoner. His episcopal brother said that the capture represented God's judgement that the king's cause was, after all, not just, and Matilda was now the true sovereign. But Matilda quarrelled with the bishop so tactlessly that he soon took a fresh consultation, and declared that God was backing Stephen after all. Matilda retired from England in 1148. In 1149 Empress Matilda's son Henry, then 16, was handed the Dukedom of Normandy by his victorious father, and prepared to launch his third invasion of England. At the height of the turmoil Stephen's heir, Eustace, died, and an agreement was reached that Henry should succeed to the throne on Stephen's death. This occurred in the following year, and the likeable young man who had been miscast as king through 19 cold winters of English misery was buried in Faversham Abbey, which he had built to supplant his predecessor Henry's monastery at Reading.

Henry II
1154-1189

Known as Fitz-Empress and nicknamed Curtmantel.

Born March 25, 1133.
Succeeded as 'King of the English, Duke of the Normans and Aquitanians, and Count of the Angevins' October 25, 1154 (having held Normandy since 1149) at the age of 21. Ultimately undisputed overlord of Ireland, Scotland and Wales.
Second cousin of his predecessor Stephen, and great-grandson of William the Conqueror.
Married in 1152 Eleanor Duchess of Aquitaine, then aged 30, immediately after her divorce from Louis VII, King of France, on the ground of consanguinity.
Children William, Henry, Matilda, RICHARD, Geoffrey, Philip, Eleanor, Joan, JOHN.
Mistresses His most serious attachment was to 'Fair Rosamund', Rosamund Clifford, whose father had changed his surname from the formidable Norman

Above *A nineteenth century engraving depicting Matilda escaping from Oxford Castle.*

Opposite top *Carved in the choir screen at York Minster, Stephen. Henry I and Richard I.*

Opposite below *A weak king, Stephen's reign was filled with anarchy. He reigned but did not rule.*

of central power in the land.

Stephen briefly reoccupied a recalcitrant Normandy in 1037, but abandoned it for ever when Empress Matilda's husband, Count Geoffrey of Anjou, took it as his share of the intended partition of English territories. At the same time Matilda invaded England itself. With a safe base within the western strongholds of Robert, Earl of Gloucester, Henry I's able illegitimate son, Matilda skirmished around the style of Fitzponce. She died in 1176.

Bastards include William Earl of Salisbury, and Geoffrey Archbishop of York.

Died at Chinon July 6, 1189 aged 56 having reigned 35 years. Buried at Fontevrault.

Profile An impressively strong-looking man, strident in his speech; a short-haired red-head with grey eyes darting from a blotchy freckled face, sporting a trimmed beard – all his predecessors since Edward the Confessor seem to have been clean-shaven, but beards were worn by English kings for the next two centuries. Henry was a man who moved with immense speed, vaulting over tables instead of going round them. His nickname 'Curtmantel' refers to the Angevin fashion of the short cloak which Henry introduced, supplanting the dusty ground-hugging cloaks which were then worn at the English Court. The flick of the short mantle as Henry cleared a hurdle or swung round a corridor/corner is a visual indication of his brisk impact.

꙳꙳꙳꙳꙳꙳꙳꙳꙳꙳꙳꙳꙳

Henry is the first of a line of 14 hereditarily related kings, who did not refer to themselves as Plantagenets until the 300th anniversary of Henry's succession, when the strain was almost extinct. Henry saw himself as an Angevin, son of the Count of Anjou whose emblem was the *plante genet*, the yellow flowering broom worn in his helmet-crest. Anjou, which is best identified as the Loire Valley with all its magnificent castles, started as a small buffer-county (like Devon) between the Celts of Brittany and the Romanized Gauls. A short time before Henry's birth at Le Mans, Anjou had incorporated Maine, which occupied a similar position with relation to Normandy as Anjou held against Brittany. This had previously been an area of dispute between the Dukes of Normandy and the Kings of France (who then only directly ruled from Paris an inland territory round the Seine, with some claim to supervision over the foreign policy of Flanders, Champagne and Burgundy). When Louis VII of France obtained his disastrously-sanctioned divorce (annulment) against Eleanor, the last Duchess of Aquitaine, and Eleanor promptly married Henry, their combined posses-

Above *Eleanor of Aquitaine, wife of Henry II used his sons against him.*

Left *Henry II, first of the Plantagenet dynasty was ruler of the Angevin empire.*

Opposite *The murder of Becket from an early illuminated manuscript. He was subsequently canonized.*

sions in France alone exceeded by far the dominions of the titular King of France; and when Henry took over England he was king of countries stretching from the Cheviots to the Pyrenees and buttressed by the Atlantic Ocean for 1000 miles. It was a domain that could accurately be called the Angevin Empire, and which was of more consequence at that time than any other state in Europe, including the Holy Roman (German) Empire.

On the death of Stephen, Henry was in Normandy, and according to the convention of the time he did not become king until his coronation in Westminster Abbey on December 19, 1154. He immediately applied himself to the painstaking organization of his new territory. He had first to demonstrate that the king was truly sovereign, and that anarchy was ended, with a determined show of strength against the maverick barons, and with the demolition of a thousand unlicensed castles which had been built during the past troubles to intimidate the countryside. Having established internal security, he

promoted domestic and foreign trade. Productivity, as measured by the national income meticulously recorded in a period of stable currency, doubled during the course of his reign. To secure a tranquil business climate and its corollary of civil freedom, he revolutionized the administration of the law, presiding often over his own courts and sending his justices out on assize. In effect he was in many cases *offering* his subjects the alternative of seeking 'the King's Justice', which was manifestly fair, rather than the loaded local justice of many existing courts. A knowledgeable lawyer himself, Henry built up the body of English Common Law (i.e., a system of common, impartial principles which carried more weight than local customs and superstitions which were still observed in the shire and manorial courts), and at the same time he began the development of the English jury system.

The fact that Henry, a foreigner from a southern civilization, could shape an acceptable and understandable corpus of law peculiar to English ideas of

liberty, and totally distinct from the Roman, institutional, law being developed within Europe, is one indication of his administrative genius. Administration was his forte. He developed a civil service which advanced the business economy of the nation, and introduced an efficient, if painful system of taxation, unashamedly using his travelling justices to collect his dues. A part of this taxation was directed to defense purposes, the feudal landowners paying *scutage* towards a paid, *ad hoc* force of mercenaries (not a standing army), rather than binding themselves to attend with men-at-arms during states of emergency, and depart, according to their rights, before the emergency was over.

Henry's major failure was his attempt to curb the power of the ecclesiastical courts. This was exemplified in his struggle with Thomas Becket. Becket had been a wild playboy crony of the king until he became Archbishop of Canterbury, and then, in somewhat ostentatious conversion, his egotism developed with a fixation on the

Above *Richard I's obsession was to regain Jerusalem. In 1189 he set out on the Third Crusade.*

Opposite *A modern view of the Abbey of Fontevrault, burial place of Henry II.*

Right *Known as Coeur de Lion, Richard is shown here in an emblematic illustration of his strength.*

Richardus.I.

maintenance of dubious ecclesiastical privilege. His unnecessary death disproportionately clouded Henry's achievement and did little for God's justice.

Henry II had a tragic private life. His cultured and vivacious queen, Eleanor, whom he had wooed with romantic rather than dynastic fervour and who gave him nine children after a late second marriage, degenerated into a foolish political intriguer, setting her sons against their father for apparently idle reasons. A rebellion in 1173 by the eldest surviving son, Henry, was crushed, and Eleanor was placed under house-arrest in Salisbury for 15 years. When young Henry died, his brothers Richard and Geoffrey conspired with the King of France against their father. The youngest brother, John, the spoiled favourite of the family, used his eye for

the main chance to support his father until a month before his death, then joined Richard and King Philip Augustus of France, and this unnatural alliance defeated Henry in battle. King Henry died deserted, exhausted and broken by grief. He was buried in his native countryside at Fontrevault Abbey on the Loire.

Richard I
1189-1199

Known as Coeur-de-Lion, Lionheart

Born at Oxford September 8, 1157.
Succeeded as Duke of Aquitaine 1172, as King of England, Duke of Normandy and Count of Anjou on July 6, 1189,

aged 31. Whatever were his tenuous claims to more of Britain, John was formal Lord of Ireland, and Richard was specifically not overlord of Scotland, having sold the right to homage for £6666.
Eldest surviving son of his predecessor Henry.
Married in Cyprus on May 12, 1191 Berengaria of Navarre.
Children none.
Died at Châlus, in Limousin, April 6, 1199, from gangrene following a wound by a cross-bolt, aged 41, having reigned ten years. Buried at Fontrevault, but his heart is buried at Rouen.
Profile tall with exceptionally long legs and arms, auburn hair and a short beard; a very handsome physique to match his bravery.

🙰🙰🙰🙰🙰🙰🙰🙰🙰

Richard was an absentee king whose influence on England arose from his neglect of it. He was a courtly musician and poet, but his great enthusiasm was for war. He was a man of high courage and an outstanding military engineer. His youth was turbulent and unpardonably disloyal, but from the age of 30 his life was dominated by the passion to regain the city of Jerusalem in what became the Third Crusade. Three months after his coronation – a ceremony which was allowed to provoke a *pogrom* of the Jews in London, and was followed by similar outbursts in Lincoln, Norwich and York – he left England, having raised for Jerusalem all the money he could in a reckless liquidation of royal perquisites. His methods were tyranical, devious and rapacious. Areas excluded from Richard's rapacity were the six counties of England which he foolishly handed over to his young and totally unreliable brother John for thorough despotic exploitation. No taxes for the Crown were levied there, and even the King's Justices were excluded from entry.

Over a year after his departure from England, Richard had got no nearer the Holy Land than Sicily. His 69-year-old mother, Eleanor of Aquitaine, travelled there to introduce to him the young princess Berengaria of Navarre (Navarre is the Basque country straddling the Pyrenees) with the suggestion that Richard should marry her. Richard dutifully agreed – since Navarre bordered the Gascony area of Aquitaine, it was a useful territory to have a claim to – and he took Berengaria on his voyage to the east. They were married, and Berengaria was crowned Queen of England, when they put ashore in Cyprus. Richard was, in fact, homosexually inclined, and he saw very little of his wife, except that he recalled

her to his bed four years later when he was accused of sodomy.

The Third Crusade was a time-consuming failure, partly because Richard was given the news that his brother John was challenging for the throne which would have come to him anyway, and Richard consequently broke off the siege of Jerusalem. Its local conclusion, three years after Richard's departure, was a national disaster and possibly ranks as England's most expensive pay-off in history for any single operation before the twentieth-century wars. Richard had

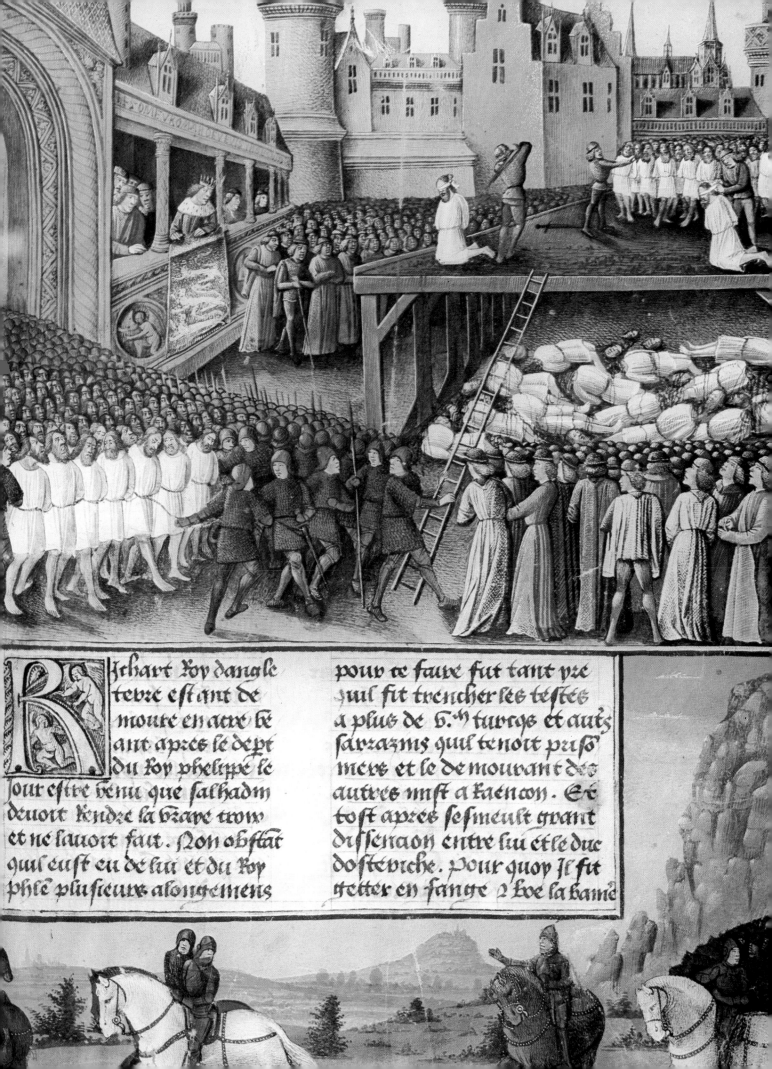

Richart Roy dangle
terre estant de
moute en aere se
ant apres le dept
du Roy phelippe le
Jour estre venu que salhadin
deuoit rendre la braye troie
et ne lauoit fait. Non obstat
quil eust eu de lui et du Roy
phle plusieurs alongemens

pour ce faire fut tant prie
quil fit trencher les testes
a plus de b.M turcos et autz
sarrazins quil tenoit prisõ
niers et le demourant des
autres mist a raēcon. Et
tost apres sesmeult grant
dissenaõ entre lui et le duc
dostriche. Pour quoy Jl fit
retter en sante ē loe la haine

Above *Winchester cathedral, the site of Richard's last appearance at home.*

mortally offended the Duke of Austria at the siege of Acre, publicly disgracing him for insubordination and having his banner trampled in the dirt. On the voyage home Richard was wrecked in the Adriatic and, taking a chance, rode through the Duke's territories on the straight route to England. He was recognized, captured, imprisoned and put up for ransom. The price was £100,000 – say £12 million in modern money, but it then represented a third of the gross national product of the country. Richard seems hardly to have been worth that, except that the alternative was John, now in alliance with Philip Augustus of France, who had accompanied Richard to the crusade but retired hurt. The most special taxes had to be collected to redeem the king, and the process took over a year. Once ransomed, Richard exhibited himself wearing his crown in Winchester Cathedral, and went straight off to Normandy for Christmas, never again visiting England. He had proved to be a most expensive king.

The country was run, and well run, by Hubert Walter, Archbishop of Canterbury and Justiciar (King's Deputy).

Richard amused himself with war in France. When a ploughman unearthed in Châlus an intricate Roman relic in gold, and his feudal overlords confiscated it, Richard considered the incident sufficiently serious to besiege Châlus and get the gold for himself. He was fatally wounded in the operation. It was a typically frivolous way to die, but Richard carried it through with a Provençal panache not too often seen among the English. He had good-naturedly congratulated the enemy crossbowman on the skill of his shooting before, miscalculating the flight, he was hit. On his deathbed he sent for the bowman, not for execution but for pardon.

John
1199-1216

Known as Lackland, also Sword-of-Lath

Born at Oxford December 24, 1167.
Succeeded on April 7, 1199 at the age of 32 as King of England, Duke of Normandy and Aquitaine, Count of Anjou, having been appointed Lord of Ireland by Henry II in 1185. William of Scotland (William the Lion) did homage making

John his overlord in 1207.
Younger brother of his predecessor Richard and, youngest son of King Henry II.
Married 1. Hadwisa (Isabella) of Gloucester (divorced 1200); 2. Isabella of Angoulême, who survived him.
Children all from the second marriage: HENRY, Richard, Joan, Isabella, Eleanor.
Bastards include another Joan, who married Llewelyn the Great, Ruler of All Wales.
Died at Newark of dysentery aggravated by over-indulgence in peaches and new cider, October 18, 1216 aged 49, having reigned 17 years. Buried at Worcester Cathedral.
Profile Medium height (5ft 6in), plump, in middle age with a bald head inside a ring of curly black hair, and fat; a broad-lipped, bland, self-concerned face; a voice menacing not through harshness but theatrically amused superiority.

ʝʧʝʧʝʧʝʧʝʧʝʧ

All kings are spoilt children, but John was the spoilt child of a family of kings. The youngest of the nine offspring of Henry II and Eleanor, he let his father down by a brief and ridiculous rule in Ireland, joined Richard in revolt when Henry was almost on his deathbed, let

down Richard when his brother became king and finally treacherously conspired with the King of France in revolt against him. He seems never to have been punished for anything, only excused as silly young John. But his people were harder than his family. His father had called him Lackland affectionately as a boy, ruefully emphasising that the private inheritable estates of the family had already been fully divided among his brothers before John was unexpectedly born to a 45-year-old queen. By standards of evolution today she would have ranked as aged 60. She lived to the actual age of 82, dominated her children like a matriarch, and besides arranging Richard's semi-forced marriage acted as Regent of England for him, at the age of 75, during his absences.

John managed to justify his nickname more obviously by losing – first through conspiracy and connivance and then through incompetence – the whole of Normandy. Anjou and Maine had already defected on the death of Richard. They chose Arthur of Brittany as their lord. John had Arthur murdered, but could not reclaim the territory. France retaliated by occupying Normandy, Anjou and Maine, and threatening Aquitaine. The Pope threatened to make the territorial situation legal and lasting by declaring John deposed and his lands forfeit to the King of France. The Pope was using this diplomatic blockbuster as a tactical weapon intended to win an entirely different victory in a struggle between the English King and the Pope over the right to appoint the Archbishop of Canterbury. A consequent military defeat in Flanders so weakened John's position that his English barons themselves called in the forces of the Dauphin of France. It was in the desultory civil war that followed – after bungling John really had lost his crown and all his treasure through not reading the tide-tables of the Wash accurately – that this ill-chosen monarch died.

He had signed *Magna Carta* under pressure. It is a document with a reputation as inflated as its signatory's body. The recalcitrant barons principally objected to demands for extra dues on the lands they held from the king which is understandable. They also objected to the king's practice of issuing writs at law which withdrew cases from trial in the baronial courts and sent them before the King's Justices, which was a self-serving and reactionary objection. But *Magna Carta* is a historically important document, and its signing a major event, because of the *significance* of the occasion of an alliance between burghers and barons against the king, and because of the significance (accorded much later) of phrases enshrining general principles of justice which the king carelessly signed.

The family life of this alleged lecherous and rapacious demon John has rarely been noticed. He wilfully divorced his first wife Hadwisa, or Isabella, of Gloucester, the grand-daughter of Robert Earl of Gloucester who was Henry I's most competent, if illegitimate, son. A year after his succession he merely chanced to see, in the course of a military campaign in France, the 12-year-old Isabella of Angoulême who was then betrothed to Hugh de Lusignan. John had enough personal charm to persuade Isabella to break this engagement, and Isabella had enough personal magnetism to keep him in bed till noon for long after their speedy marriage, which culminated in the crowning in Westminster Abbey of the 12-year-old as Queen of England. It was seven years before they had their first child, but it is interesting to see the positions of state which their offspring took up in the world. John was not such an international ogre that kings did not want to marry his daughters. His son Henry became Henry III. The next son, Richard, was Earl of Cornwall and King of the Romans. John's daughter Joan married Alexander II, King of the Scots. His daughter Isabella, married Frederick II of Hohenstaufen and Sicily, Holy Roman Emperor. His youngest daughter Eleanor married Simon de Montfort. And an illegitimate daughter, Joan, married Llywelyn the Great, Ruler of All Wales. As for Isabella of Angoulême, she finally betrayed John politically before he died. She went to France, and as soon as her husband was dead she married her first love, Hugh de Lusignan. Later she took the veil. Her son Henry was to be England's next monarch, and he was only nine when he succeeded to the throne. In his minority, the country was well governed by a regent, and the young boy was educated by priests until he was old enough to take the throne.

Top Magna Carta, *signed in 1215 and containing 63 clauses in all is one of the most momentous documents in English history.*

Above *The field of Runnymede believed to be the place where John set his seal to Magna Carta. Had he refused, civil war was threatened.*

48

Henry III
1216-1272

Born at Winchester, October 1, 1207.
Succeeded as King of England and Duke of Aquitaine, October 19, 1216 at the age of nine.
Eldest son of his predecessor John.
Married in 1236 Eleanor of Provence, then aged 14, who survived him and died 1291.
Children EDWARD, Margaret, Beatrice, Edmund, who all survived him, and Richard, John, Katherine, William and Henry, who all died young.
Died naturally at Westminster on November 16, 1272 aged 65, having reigned 56 years. Buried at Westminster Abbey.
Profile Short stature; always plump; dark bobbed hair and beard which went prematurely grey; a kindly face and a gaze taking in only a short perspective in every sense; the left eyelid was noticeably drooping.

❦❦❦❦❦❦❦❦❦❦❦❦❦

Henry had a domestic character and artistic interests. Statesmanship was beyond him, and drove him to a desperation of error. He would have excelled as a cultured country gentleman, interested in the lives of everyone on the estate but flummoxed by an agrarian dispute with another country gentleman, and impelled into extravagant intrigues to forestall the innocent ambitions of a parish council. In this sense he was a bad king. In another sense he was good for the country. His genuine passion for the arts, and his ability as Royal Patron to foster them was great. His debts were huge, as he said, 'By God's head I owe 300,000 marks'. He endowed the land with public munificence and a richening influx of artists and craftsmen who basked in the fashionable appreciation that royalty sponsored. It also gave us a Westminster Abbey rebuilt as we largely know it today. This is Henry's masterpiece, and the building can be well judged from the interior. Later accretions rob its distant impact of the airy vitality with which the Early English style replaced the stolidity of the Norman, and which is best seen now in the

contemporary Salisbury Cathedral.

Politically, Henry was a failure, and may therefore be cited as the illustrative personality condemning hereditary monarchy. But morals are part of politics. And Henry – son of that John who had demanded the flesh of the wives of his nobility with a brutal insistence unparalleled since the decadent Roman Empire – was himself a model husband and father, ecstatically wrapped up in his family. He was, too, the grandson of Henry II and the father of Edward I, politically two of the most capable monarchs in English history. Perhaps Henry's trouble was that he had inadequate training. He was king at the age of nine, and from that time on he was long in the hands of priests who gave no instruction in kingship, though at the same time the country was very adequately governed by a regent. Trouble intensified when Henry declared himself of age to rule.

Above *An excellent example of Early English architecture, Salisbury Cathedral also houses a copy of* Magna Carta.

It fell to Henry to confirm formally the decline of English possessions in France. In 1268 he resigned Normandy (which he had never controlled) in return for a subsidy from the King of France. Anjou had been lost by his father, King John, and in the course of his reign Henry had to do homage to the King of France for Guienne, the major part of the Duchy of Aquitaine. This diminution of the responsibilities of the English throne – virtually the extinction of the Angevin Empire – has been generally welcomed by English historians as concentrating the interests of the king and the activities of the better type of English barons on the development of England as a country of individual character and customs. Yet the English continued to

expend much warlike energy on attempting to retain the old imperialism. And, if they had succeeded, a Franco-British Empire – which was the logical development of the Angevin Empire – might have been a strong pacifying influence in Europe for centuries to come. It would have avoided the culturally destructive and financially horrendous distraction of the Hundred Years War and the 50 later years, ending at Waterloo, when England was at war with France.

Henry, though English born and bred (and early deserted by his mother), had a remarkably European orientation. His brother, Richard of Cornwall, became King of the Romans, and his son Edmund was given the emptier title of

Opposite *The tomb of Henry III with the effigy in gilt bronze.*

Below *Henry III is depicted here at the battle of Lewes, where de Montfort defeated Henry.*

King of Sicily (which Henry's Angevin brother-in-law later exploited far more fully). His sister Isabella married the Emperor Frederick II. His sister Joan and his daughter Margaret married successive kings of the Scots, while his half-sister Joan married Llywelyn the Great. His daughter Beatrice married the Duke of Brittany, who also held the English earldom of Richmond. His wife Eleanor was one of four sisters who became queens – of France, England, Rome and Sicily. (The kings of France and Sicily were brothers, as were the kings of England and Rome – a remarkable consanguinity with four sister queens).

Henry certainly did not accept the loss of empire, and spent much time and money fighting, or negotiating, and sometimes just artistically dawdling, with his brother-in-law Louis IX of France. As an absentee tax-gatherer, and moreover a taxing-master regulating the collection of dues for the Pope, he did not increase his popularity at home.

His expensive administration stuck the more sharply in English throats when it was seen to be increasingly carried out by the Italians from Rome, Provençals from his wife's family, and even the young Frenchmen from Poitou who were Henry's half-brothers. The recalcitrant nobility, excluded by foreigners from government, and resisting high taxes for foreign indulgences as well as ecclesiastical foundations, were led in revolt, ironically, by another foreigner, Simon de Montfort, who had inherited his earldom of Leicester and subsequently married the King's sister Eleanor. Montfort engineered the convention at Oxford called *The Mad Parliament'*, where armed barons intimidated the king into governing by a representative Council of State balancing the royal needs and the national interests.

In subsequent sparring Henry himself, not Montfort, called the knights of the shire to Windsor. The two sides were preparing for battle, and two years of civil war ensued. They ended with

Montfort's capture of Henry and his heir, Edward, and the calling of the first true embryo Parliament in London in 1265, where bishops, barons, knights and – at last – the burghers of the towns all met. Later that year Edward escaped from imprisonment, and Simon de Montfort was defeated and killed in the subsequent battle of Evesham. Edward exploited his victory with an effective military campaign against the suddenly unorganized rebel barons. Surprisingly, in a man who had been pictured as an effete, yet dangerous, tyrant, Henry revised his attitude after the shock of the civil war. He trimmed his demands and saw his reign end in unaccustomed stability. He attended the completion of Westminster Abbey, re-interred the body of Edward the Confessor in a new shrine, and was himself buried in the Confessor's former coffin in Westminster, where his bronze effigy now stands.

Edward I
1272-1307

(Known as Edward Longshanks)

Born at Westminster Palace June 18, 1239.

Succeeded on November 16, 1272 as King of England and Lord of Gascony (a diminution of Aquitaine to its northern territory; later he was accepted as Duke of Aquitaine after paying homage to the King of France); Overlord of Ireland, for which he paid homage to the Pope; Overlord of Scotland (for which he refused to pay homage to the Pope) and King of Scotland from 1296; Overlord of Wales, and King after 1282, when Wales was annexed into the territories of the English Crown.

Eldest son of his predecessor Henry.

Married 1. in 1254 when he was 15 and she was 10, Eleanor of Castile, daughter of Ferdinand III King of Castile and Leon; she died 1290. 2. Margaret of France, daughter of Philip III (Philip the Bold) King of France, and sister of the then regnant Philip IV (Philip the Fair); she survived him and died 1317.

Children of Eleanor, Eleanor, Joan (died 1265), John, Henry, Julian (Katherine), Joan of Acre (born 1271,

Died 1307), Alphonso, Isabel, Margaret, Berengaria, Mary, Alice, Elizabeth, EDWARD, Beatrice, Blanche; of Margaret, Thomas, Edmund, Eleanor.

Died of dysentery at Burgh-by-Sands (past Carlisle, on the Solway Firth) on July 6, 1307 aged 68, having reigned 35 years. Buried in Westminster Abbey.

Profile Very much in the cast of his grandfather's brother, Richard Coeur-de-Lion, Edward was outstandingly tall and lithe with long arms and legs. His hair was silver-blond until it went surprisingly dark in adolescence and eventually turned bright milk-white. He wore it at shoulder-length and kept a clipped beard. His speech was impulsive and indistinct. Though he had a self-depreciative sense of humour, his face was notably lean and stern; he inherited his father's drooping eyelid. His sparse cultural interests were music and architecture.

ᑭᕈᒖᕈᒖᕈᒖᕈᒖᕈᒖᕈᒖᕈᒖᕈ

Edward was, in the eyes of his father Henry III, literally a Godsend, since Henry, through lack of desire had delayed his marriage until he was 28, and was then disappointed and indeed alarmed when three years passed before Eleanor was pregnant. The boy was named after Henry's patron saint, King Edward the Confessor, whom the Pope had canonized with that title less than a century after his death. (Before Edward 'the First' there were, in fact, three Kings of England named Edward – the Elder, the Martyr and the Confessor).

In the same manner as Edward's own nomination of his heir as Prince of Wales – Wales being disputable territory at the time – Henry had created Edward Lord of Gascony at the age of 12. Two years later, as part of his busy intriguing between the desultory lootings of a minor military campaign in France, Henry arranged Edward's dynastic marriage. Alfonso X had recently acceded to the combined thrones of Castile and Leon. Alfonso had claims on Gascony. Edward was betrothed to Alfonso's half-sister Eleanor of Castile, daughter of his lately-deceased father Ferdinand III, and by this alliance took over Alfonso's claim to Gascony. Edward sailed to Bordeaux and went on to Burgos, and the boy-and-girl marriage took place. It was an exceedingly fruitful union and a rare, devoted companionship. Eleanor

travelled constantly with her husband and bore him campaign-children in Rouen, Acre in the Holy Land, Bordeaux and Caernarvon. Most of their 16 babies were girls, and some survived them – though Joan of Acre died in the same year as her father. But Edward's eventual heir was his 14th child, born in the 30th year of the marriage. Edward, however, continued to beget children well into his sixties.

Long before he was 20, Edward was overlord of Ireland and responsible for the good order of Gascony and of Wales, where he ruled the Marches as Earl of Chester. He was not conspicuously successful as a general, and somewhat overplayed the role of a spoilt and roistering princeling predominantly interested in the ostentatious combats of set tournaments – though these demanded high skill and personal bravery: many dozens of knights could be killed during a single staged jousting-match, and there were no favours for princes. But when he was 24, though he had originally admitted the justice of his godfather's, Simon de Montfort's, constitutional struggle against King Henry III, Edward rallied to support his father. As the leading general on the royalist side in the civil war, he eventually defeated Montfort. His subsequent pacification of England was statesmanlike and authoritative, as High Steward he was virtually his father's Regent after 1268. But from 1270 until 1274 he was abroad on a crusade to the Holy Land, followed by a state tour of Europe and a reconquest of troubled Gascony. However, he had succeeded unchallenged to the English throne on his father's death in 1272.

Edward was a mature sovereign at the age of 35 with an extreme devotion to personal and political integrity. His abiding principle, which is carved on his tomb in Westminster Abbey, was *pactum serva*, 'keep your word', and it is fair to say that he mainly kept this code except in the numerous exigencies of war. Edward devoted his long reign to the shaping of England as an integrated state of repute within Christendom, and even beyond: he exchanged personal missions with the King of Persia, a Mongol Tartar and not a Moslem. In

Opposite *Tomb of Eleanor of Castile.*

this quest to create a state he faced difficult local problems which he met by strong and arbitrary means. Controversy is still valid over his treatment of the Scots, the Welsh and the Jews.

In his attitude to the outlying territories of England Edward was a strictly conformist feudal monach of his time. Where he paid homage to a higher lord, he expected strong fealty from his own feudal dependents in turn. When he faced running revolt, and finally a war for outright independence in tribal Wales – then a far smaller pocket of territory than its geographical area today – he occupied Gwynedd, Anglesey and Dyfed after a pincer operation from the land and the sea, and annexed Wales to the English crown. The last Welsh Prince of Wales, Llywelyn ap Gruffydd, died in battle, and Edward symbolically presented to the Welsh people his own baby son, born in Caernarvon, but did not create him Prince of Wales until he was 16. Ironically, Wales bequeathed to England a powerful weapon of future British imperialism: the Welsh long-bow and Welsh bowmen using it. Edward's appreciation of this weapon and his deliberate encouragement of its use throughout England made the long-bow arrow, which could penetrate four inches of oak, the most accurate and efficient weapon before the development of gunpowder.

The conquest of Wales did not bring instant pacification. Too much unregulated power had to be delegated to the despotic Lords Marcher, whose vast estates ran from Chester to Monmouth and far to the west, and whose bloody quarrels eventually toppled the royal dynasty. War in Scotland was no more constructively successful. The kingdom of Scotland, centred on the fat Lothian lands of old Northumbria rather than on the Highland glens, had become deliberately orientated towards the Norman-Saxon civilisation of territorial and ecclesiastical feudalism, rather than observing the tribalism of the clans and the simpler church administration of Saint Columba. Its centre tended to be Sassenach Edinburgh rather than the Celtic capital at Scone. On the death of Alexander III of Scotland, a second cousin of Edward's who had married Edward's sister Margaret, the crown of Scotland passed to Alexander's granddaughter Margaret, 'the Maid of

Opposite above *Edward I and his parliament. A mature sovereign at 35, he promoted a great awakening of nationalism in England.*

Opposite below *Balliol revolted after being nominated to the Scottish throne. He lost this battle to Edward, who took the throne under his jurisdiction.*

Right *The coronation stone of Scotland was removed after Balliol's defeat and placed beneath the coronation chair in Westminster Abbey.*

Below *Edward I, a fine combination of soldier and statesman, he was dedicated to English interests, and was effective in pursuing them.*

Norway', at the age of three. In 1290 Edward carried through the betrothal of the young Queen Margaret to his own heir Edward, when both were aged six. An eventual marriage would have led to a peaceful union of the lands of England and Scotland. But the Maid died almost immediately, shipwrecked on a voyage to Scotland for her coronation. There was a multiple dispute over the succession. King Edward, as overlord, stepped in to arbitrate with a remarkably balanced Commission which deliberated for 18 months, and awarded the throne to John Balliol, who paid homage along with the Scottish peers.

Edward's subsequent colonialization of Scotland led to a revolt which the English king overcame. In 1296 he deposed Balliol, proclaimed himself King of Scotland, and carried off the Coronation Stone of Scone and the Great Seal. In the following year Sir William Wallace organized a fresh revolt but was eventually defeated. He retired to France, and after five years returned to wage guerilla warfare, but he was captured and executed. In 1306 Robert Bruce was crowned at Scone as King of Scots, and the *de facto* Scottish monarchy began anew. In the ensuing war he was at first defeated. But it was while Edward I was leading a further campaign to crush his resurgence that the English king died at Burgh by Sands having reigned 35 years.

Continuous warfare on the part of Edward – in Gascony and Flanders and on the French coast as well as his own borders – led to a continuous lack of funds. He made a number of questionable impositions on the country and borrowed heavily from the Jews, the only section of the population who were then allowed to make heavy financial loans. Because of this monopoly and their restricted social function, which had barred them from productive enterprise, the Jews charged high rates of interest and, using other expertise in their role as currency manipulators, were involved in the common crime of clipping the coinage. This was the most flagrant inflationary act possible at a time when gold or silver coin had a value corresponding to its initial weight in precious metal.

Soon after his accession, Edward passed legislation banning usury and encouraging the Jews to take up productive occupations. But, in the conditions of the time, there was more profit to be made out of the old vocation of the Jews and the temptations which it provided. Over the next 15 years they did not move into agriculture or manufacture – nor did they get any local encouragement. Their unpopularity, heightened by sensational charges alleging the ritual murder of Christian children, increased in authoritarian circles when Edward's rare 'Parliaments' realized that the king was still borrowing from the Jews instead of making concessions in return for parliamentary consent to taxation. In 1290 Edward reacted by approving an ordinance expelling the Jews from England. Consequently, in 1295, he was forced to call what is termed the first Model Parliament, summoning the representatives of the towns and rural areas as well as the lords spiritual and temporal. He wanted support to raise taxes.

With such an apparent detailed personal history of aggression, it is difficult to justify summarily the reputation which Edward earned in his own lifetime and later as a lawgiver and administrator, with the interests of the people of England truly at his heart. He is acknowledged as having enlarged 'freedom from fear' by firm extension of public order; as having rewritten the land laws (as much in the interests of the tenants against the encroachment of the Church and other spreading landlords as to clarify his own position as primary patron); as having reshaped the organization of the law courts; redefined the military obligations of the people with a view to speedier reaction in emergency; and as having accepted, however reluctantly, the broad principle of parliamentary consent to national taxation.

He was a man who chose to lead by personal example. In his youth he made a trunk road safe by challenging the leader of the harassing highwaymen, an outlawed knight, to personal combat, and beating him. In his old age he mourned his dead wife – the Eleanor Crosses erected from Grantham to the old Charing Cross were her visible memorial – and yet, in the cause of national diplomacy, he sealed a necessary peace treaty by marrying the French King's sister. He stamped the seal by fathering three strong children in his seventh decade.

Edward II
1307-1327

Known as Edward of Caernarvon

Born at Caernarvon April 25, 1284.
Succeeded on July 7, 1307 at age 23 as King of England, titular Overlord of Ireland and Scotland, and Duke of Aquitaine, having been briefly Regent of England in 1297, and Prince of Wales and Earl of Chester from 1301.
Eldest surviving son (actually fourth son and 14th child) of his predecessor Edward.
Married in January 1308 Isabella ('She-Wolf') of France then aged 16, daughter of King Philip IV (Philip the Fair) of France. She was conspicuously unfaithful to him, militarily defeated him, survived him, and died in 1358 after 27 years in seclusion.
Children EDWARD, John, Eleanor, Joanna.
Formally abdicated at Kenilworth January 20, 1327 after having been deposed by Parliament, aged 42 having reigned 19 years.
Died in agony, murdered at Berkeley Castle on September 22, 1327, aged 43. Buried in Gloucester Cathedral.
Profile an alert, mobile, handsome face conveying a shallow nature. His bright auburn hair was bobbed and rolled in a natural curl. At most times he wore a beard slightly pointed, but he died wearing only rough stubble. In his last prison cell in Gloucestershire, where he was mocked and crowned with straw, his warders shaved him with cold water from the Severn. He only commented: 'Whether you will or no, I have warm tears for my beard'. His body was athletic and strong. His taste was for amusement, often in low company and aspiring to nothing more cultural than pitch-and-toss. He was interested in play-acting and could write touching, if self-indulgent, verse.

༄༄༄༄༄༄༄༄༄༄༄༄

Edward II was an unreformed Prince Hal with no Falstaff to spark sympathetic human depth and no Lord Chief Justice to provoke, however priggishly, a sense of status and responsibility. His mother died, after a long illness, when he was six. Over the following years his

Above *A modern view of Caernarvon Castle, birthplace, April 25, 1284, of Edward II.*

Right *This portrait of Edward II confirms him to be the possessor of traditional Plantagenet good looks.*

father was fighting in three countries until he married again after his 60th birthday and became absorbed in his new family; but he took young Edward with him to meet Parliament and to command a division during one Scottish campaign, and gave him some experience at presiding over his council. The fact remained that Edward was a lonely boy, until a playmate was deliberately sought for him. The choice of this companion was the most fateful single decision in his life. The French boy Piers Gaveston, son of a valiant knight from Gascony, duplicated Edward's own bent towards frivolity so accurately that between them they multiplied their mutual faults through resonance. They grew up as an uncontrolled, wilful and witty pair of pranksters, democratically finding their pleasure in any class of company that was available; brave, strong, dissipated and extremely irresponsible. Edward's social perspective was filled by Gaveston, and while Gaveston was available he wanted nothing but a social life. No reliable suggestion of any homosexual inclinations has been advanced by the calumniators of these laughing idlers, in spite of the deep enmity which the relationship inspired among the English nobility.

King Edward I was himself perturbed at Gaveston's psychological domination of his son, and on his last campaign he ordered the Gascon's banishment. A month after his father's death Edward II brought back Piers Gaveston, made him Earl of Cornwall—a title normally restricted to the royal family and then coveted by Margaret of France for her first-born son who was the Heir Presumptive—and married him to the richest lady in England, his niece Margaret of Gloucester, daughter of his sister Joan of Acre. He then appointed Gaveston Regent of England while he went to France to marry the king's daughter, 16-year-old Isabella, to whom he had been betrothed for ten years. She later arranged his death.

Aristocratic opposition to the favours given to the young *parvenu* Gaveston was total. It was led, constitutionally, within the council, by Thomas of Lancaster, a savage and active Marcher Lord who held five earldoms and was both the cousin of the king (their grandfather was Henry III) and of the queen (through Lancaster's mother, Blanche of Navarre). It is significant that the earls who decided Edward's fate were mainly Marcher Lords–Lancaster, Gloucester, Pembroke and finally Mortimer, Earl of March. Within a year of his accession Edward was forced by the Council to deprive Gaveston of the earldom of Cornwall and to decree his exile. He promptly appointed Gaveston his Deputy in Ireland and assigned him an income to match.

Within another year Gaveston was back in court, virtually managing the government of the country and spending revenue with monstrous extravagance. As a consequence both the king and Gaveston were pushed aside by the appointment of 21 Lords Ordainers to manage the economy both of the country and the court. The first stage of the struggle of the earls against the playboy king ended with armed conflict, Lancaster's capture of Gaveston, and Gaveston's prompt execution.

The reign was only four years old. The gloom of Edward's personal life was lightened by the birth of a son and heir, and by the Pope's warm insistence that Edward should confiscate the English treasure of the order of the Knights Templar, which Rome, prompted by the King of France, was determined to crush. But state affairs intervened. On June 24, 1314 King Edward, fighting with courage and some skill, made the English loss of Scotland irretrievable for three centuries with his defeat at Bannockburn. Robert Bruce's brother Edward completed Edward's colonial discomfiture by invading Ulster and harrying Ireland out of all prospect of prosperity or culture for many generations.

The immediate result of Bannockburn was that Edward II was forced into a confrontation with Lancaster, who took over formal government as leader of the Lords Ordainers. Over the next six years Edward, comparatively powerless but with a seeming compulsion for extravagant devotion, cultivated as Gaveston's successors in his heart Hugh, Lord le Despenser, an old friend, and his son, also Hugh le Despenser. He made the younger Despenser his Court Chamberlain and married him to another daughter of Joan of Acre, once Countess of Gloucester. This marriage brought in as dowry the county of Glamorgan, and involved the younger Despenser and his rapacious

Charles le bel recevant la Reine d'Angleterre

father in endless controversy over territory in Wales with the Earl of Lancaster and Roger Mortimer, Earl of March.

In 1321 the Mortimer-Lancaster alliance was strong enough to force the king to banish the Despensers. But Edward sprang back, seized his opportunities, captured Mortimer and sent him to the Tower of London, then fought and captured Lancaster and had him executed. The Despensers were reinstated, but in their thick-skinned greed they could not expect to find a single friend outside the king's chamber. By this time Roger Mortimer and Queen Isabella had become physical lovers. In 1324 Isabella contrived Mortimer's

Above *Isabella, wife of Edward II followed her lover Mortimer to France in 1325.*

Right *An alabaster effigy of Edward II in Gloucester Cathedral.*

escape out of the Tower of London into France, and followed him the next year, afterwards gaining possession there of her son Edward, the heir to the throne. In September 1326 Isabella, Mortimer, the young Prince and his uncle the Earl of Kent, the 23-year-old son of Edward I and Margaret of France, landed in Suffolk. Barons and burghers hurried to their standard. The newly-

raised army marched to the west, proclaiming the Prince as governor of the country. Edward could find no-one to support him and, taking refuge among the Welsh was contemptuously handed over to his wife. Both Despensers were hanged, and Edward was imprisoned in Kenilworth in the doubtful care of his cousin Henry, Earl of Lancaster, younger brother of the executed Thomas of Lancaster.

Soon after the New Year, Parliament met in Westminster Palace and declared the young Prince Edward king. A shady political supporter of Queen Isabella, Adam Orlton, Bishop of Hereford, led a deputation to Edward II in Kenilworth and announced that his younger children would be killed unless he renounced the throne. On January 20, 1327 he formally abdicated. Isabella and her lover Mortimer then strove to procure his death by some method which would not show the marks of violence, and sent him to a succession of distant dungeons. But Edward's strong physical and psychological constitution refused to submit to degradation, deprivation and exposure to disease. On September 22, 1327, on the orders of the Bishop of Hereford, Edward was savagely killed by the insertion of a red-hot iron bar into his bowels.

Edward III
1327-1377

Born at Windsor November 13, 1312. **Succeeded** on January 20, 1327 at age 14 as King of England, Duke of Aquitaine and Overlord of Ireland. He solemnly resigned his claim to Scotland in 1327 yet exacted homage from Edward Balliol in 1333. He formally styled himself King of France in January 1340, and quartered the French lilies with the English lions on his shield from that date.
Elder son of his predecessor Edward, who was still living at his accession.
Married at York in January 1328, at age 15, the bride being 13, Philippa, daughter of William III Count of Hainault in Flanders. She died after 41 years in 1369.
Children Edward (the Black Prince), Isabella, Joanna, William, Lionel, John, (of Gaunt), Blanche, Edmund, Mary, Margaret, William (who died young, like his other son William), Thomas.
Mistress Alice Perrers, among many, particularly in his later life.
Bastards by Alice Perrers, Nicholas Litlington, Abbot of Westminster, and two daughters.
Died of a circulatory disorder hastened by a stroke at Sheen on June 21, 1377 aged 64, having reigned 50 years. Buried in Westminster Abbey.
Profile medium height, handsome and well-proportioned with a very striking royal 'presence'. Athletic, a keen sportsman and jouster, and a good sailor. His straight fair hair was bobbed

Right *King Edward III, from a window in St Mary's Church, Shrewsbury.*

Below *Windsor Castle, birthplace of Edward III, November 13, 1312.*

edvard̃ tci̇ rex anglı

at the neck and he wore his beard spade-shaped, but not so long as in the magnificently stylized effigy on his tomb in Westminster Abbey, nor was his hair so profuse. He went bald with age.

❀❀❀❀❀❀❀❀❀❀❀❀❀

Son of an ostentatious royal failure and child of a broken marriage, of which he was constantly and shamefully reminded in his most impressionable years, Edward III still emerged as a king of glamour through half a century of swelling national prestige. Part of this achievement was due to his personality. Part followed from the evolution of an English sense of nationalism, precocious in Europe, the foundations of which lay in the solid work of his grandfather Edward I and in the country's irritated sense of the frustration of uncreative idleness experienced under Edward II. The historian G. M. Trevelyan has observed that, for balanced libertarian development, it is not good to have an unbroken succession of 'great' rulers. The problem this creates is one of dependance and passivity.

As a boy of 14 Edward was the puppet of his mother and Mortimer when they landed from France at Orwell Haven and then hanged one Despenser from a gibbet 50 feet high and proclaimed the lad as England's guardian. After his official accession, Isabella and her lover still controlled both the government and the royal revenue. They signed a costly treaty with Isabella's last surviving brother, King Charles IV of France, which was doubly humiliating by reason of Charles's almost immediate death, giving Edward a sound claim to the French throne. The treaty with France was followed by Edward's renunciation of all claims to Scotland. The Mortimer-Isabella régime was resisted by the king's uncles, Henry Earl of Lancaster, Thomas Earl of Norfolk and Edmund Earl of Kent. But their opposition was uncoordinated, and the queen and her lover were able to have Edmund of Kent judicially murdered.

However, Edward, newly married and, rising 17, already a father, felt competent enough to assert himself. When a Parliament was called at Nottingham, he penetrated the castle at night with a few friends, plucked Mortimer out of his mother's bed, and had him judicially murdered too – in formal terms

Above *The raising of the siege of the ancient city of Orleans marked a turning point for the French during the Hundred Years' War.*

Below *Joan of Arc, sometimes called the Maid of Orleans, was the inspiration behind the French victory at Orleans. She was later executed by the English.*

Above *Edward III leading his troops against the French during the Siege of Tournai.*

Below *Crécy was the first significant English victory of the Hundred Years' War which dominated Europe.*

Mortimer was hanged at Tyburn following an arbitrary sentence of death as an enemy of the state pronounced through an Act of Attainder. Isabella was confined for the remaining 28 years of her life in Castle Rising, in Norfolk. Edward quickly developed, through temperament and opportunity as the flower of chivalry and the protagonist of that that romantic-conventional, foolhardy-mercenary ideal of courtly piracy which still tints nostalgic Christendom with its rosy myth. He set out to prove himself first by renewing the war against the Scots. He defeated them, by backing a rival king, and exacted fresh homage from the Pretender Edward Balliol. Philip VI of France, Edward's second cousin, supported Scotland, received the refugee King David II and his queen (who was Edward's sister Joan), cancelled Edward's long-concealed title to Aquitaine, and prepared an invasion of England. Edward retaliated by claiming the throne of France.

The Hundred Years War had started. Its total span was 115 years until 1453. Edward's objective was (besides honour, which was an important psychological drive) the retention and expansion of the wool trade with Flanders which had boomed since his marriage to Philippa of Hainault; the retention and expansion of the wine trade with Gascony; and the opportunities for extended feudal dues and sheer plunder through military aggression which he glimpsed along with the restless and comparatively co-ordinated English aristocracy. In a significant early naval battle he destroyed almost the entire French fleet off Sluys in 1340. He justified and glorified the English concentration on the use of professional long-bowmen at Crécy in 1346. And at the same time Queen Philippa, fighting independently in the north, used the same arm to defeat the invading Scots at Neville's Cross and capture King David II of Scotland.

In the following year Edward starved Calais into surrender. Queen Philippa's intercession with him not to hang the capitulating burghers of Calais who had grossly annoyed the king by holding out so long is not entirely fiction; but the story may have been wilfully inflated at the time into psychological propaganda for chivalric warfare. It is, however, true that before the main struggle started Edward made a genuine 'chivalrous' offer to the King of France to settle the dispute by single combat, or alternatively by a battle between 100 picked knights on either side. The offer was ignored. But Edward did fight in single combat with a French champion outside the walls of Calais in 1349. Romance and war were not then incompatible.

In 1348 Europe temporarily abandoned warfare under the affliction of the economic consequences of bubonic plague – the Black Death which in England alone killed a million-and-a-half people, over one-third of the population. The consequences of a depleted national labour force demanding higher rates of pay were to be momentous, as were the continuous concessions diminishing the royal prerogative which Edward was forced to grant in order to raise money for his wars. Serious fighting was renewed in 1355, and in the following year Edward's son the Black Prince captured the French King John II after the victory at Poitiers. This was the peak of the long confrontation, and Edward's military fortune slumped to disaster over the next 20 years. But he had had his Roman triumph. If he wanted visible proof of temporal glory he could display the King of the Scots confined in the Tower and the King of France at Windsor Castle. The former was a prisoner for 11 years, the latter for eight years including an interval to go home to collect his ransom. Ransom was fixed respectively at 100,000 marks and the incredible sum of three million gold crowns, but very little was paid on either account, and King John, having honourably returned when he failed to fetch his price, died in captivity.

By the temporary Peace of Bretigny in 1360 Edward renounced his claim to the French throne and was awarded vastly extended territory round Aquitaine together with the bastion of Calais. But war was renewed eight years later, and Edward resumed his title as King of France. The pendulum, however, had swung. Edward's effectiveness was prematurely senile, and his administration was only worsened by the destructiveness of his sons, whose names still have a false glamour in modern ears because of the influence of Froissart and Shakespeare. King Edward III was the first English monarch to grant dukedoms involving

English territory, though he and his ancestors had accepted the French titles of Duke of Aquitaine, or even Normandy. Edward made his heir, Edward, Duke of Cornwall as well as Prince of Wales, Prince of Aquitaine and Earl of Chester.

The next son who reached maturity, Lionel of Antwerp, was Duke of Clarence and Earl of Ulster. John of Gaunt (Antwerp and Ghent, the birthplaces of these two boys, are a reminder of Edward's close connection with Flanders through his queen) became Duke of Lancaster through his first marriage and lodged a woundingly expensive claim to be King of Castile and Leon through his second. Edward of Langley was Duke of York, and Thomas of Woodstock Duke of Gloucester, the first creation of these quasi-royal titles. Edward Prince of Wales, who was never called the Black Prince until two centuries after his death, earned the description through his temperament rather than the colour of his armour. After winning his spurs at Crécy at the age of 16 he became a competent general, but a ruthless victor, a tyrannous overlord and an ill-equipped expansionist. He was, in brief, one of the cruel Plantagenets, and might have indelibly altered the pace of English evolution. But he contracted a wasting disease during his campaigns and, after long debility, died a year before his father. John of Gaunt was a busy but short-sighted intriguer who would have given his eye-teeth to have anticipated Shakespeare's creation for him of the theme 'This blessed plot, this earth, this realm, this England' – but never had the vision. The total achievement of King Edward III and his five ducal sons was that, at Edward's funeral, little remained of all his French conquests except the fortresses at Bayonne, Bordeaux and Calais.

After Queen Philippa's death in 1369 Edward, whose libido was stronger than his martial stamina, resorted to a succession of mistresses. The most notable was Alice Perrers. In a summertime at Sheen, deserted by his family and irritated by priapism and shingles in addition to serious arterial trouble, Edward had his terminal stroke. Alice Perrers looked at the paralyzed hulk, stripped the rings off his fingers, and left him. A priest found him hours later and heard him say *Miserere Jesu*

Opposite *Life in the Middle Ages from a contemporary manuscript.*

Above *An etching of Philippa of Hainault, wife of Edward III.*

before he died. He had won famous victories but had only three castles left to show for them. At home he had rebuilt Windsor Castle and recreated the legendary feats there of King Arthur's circle of the Round Table with his institution of the Order of the Garter. But that version of the founding is unsubstantiated which says that he innocently picked up the garter of the Countess of Salisbury at a Court dance, and responded to cynically raised eyebrows around him with the priggish retort: 'Evil be to him that evil thinks'. What is certified is the report that he violently ravished Katherine, Countess of Salisbury during an overnight stay at her castle in the middle of a campaign against the Scots, her husband the Earl of Salisbury being then one of his principal generals abroad. For a dubbed knight, but especially for a king, it was not easy to be chivalrous all the time.

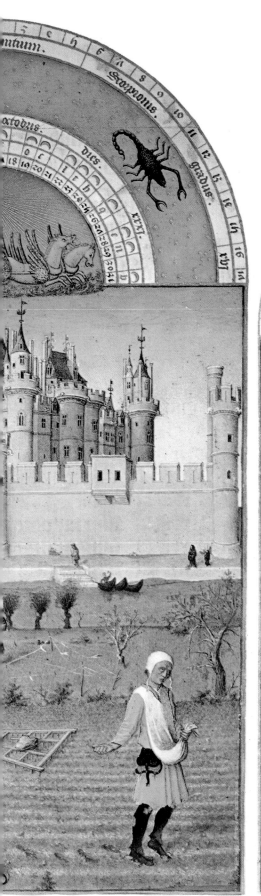

Richard II
1377-1399

Known as Richard of Bordeaux

Born at Bordeaux January 6, 1367.
Succeeded as King of England, Wales and Ireland on June 21, 1377 at the age of ten.
Grandson of his predecessor Edward, being only surviving son (of two sons) of Edward Prince of Wales (the Black Prince). Doubly related to King Edward I, being great-great-grandson on his father's side and great-grandson on his mother's side. (The Black Prince married Joan, 'Fair Maid of Kent', daughter of that Edmund Earl of Kent whom Queen Isabella and Roger Mortimer had executed in 1330. Edmund had been born to Edward I and Margaret of France when Edward was 64 years old). Richard was also the great-grandson of Philip the Bold of France, and through a Welsh strain inherited the genes of Llywelyn and King John.
Married in January 1382 when the bride and groom were both 15, 1. Anne of Bohemia, daughter of the Emperor Charles IV and sister of King Wenceslaus of Bohemia. She died in June 1394; 2. in September 1396, when the bride was aged nine and Richard 29, Isabella of Valois, daughter of King Charles VI of France. She survived him, remarried, and died in childbirth in 1409.
Children none.
Abdicated September 29, 1399 and was deposed by Parliament the same day, at the age of 32, having reigned 22 years. Died early in 1400 (reported as on February 14, 1400) at Pontefract, either of self-starvation or murder by his gaolers. Buried at Langley. His body was removed by Henry V in 1413 to lie with his queen Anne in the joint tomb still to be seen in Westminster Abbey.
Profile Almost 6ft tall, always handsome, having a very fair complexion with profuse golden hair worn wide over his ears. Towards the end of his short life he wore a small trimmed beard. He was garrulous, highly-strung and quick-tempered, and was artistically cultured in many spheres.

Richard was born in Aquitaine, where his father, the Black Prince, was prince-regnant, and at the age of four he was brought to England on the death of his elder brother Edward. His father died when he was nine, and Richard was created Prince of Wales and Duke of Cornwall. Next year he was king. Succeeding to the throne at the age of ten, he submitted to the government of a regency council. But he showed his own initiative and leadership when, at 14, he personally conciliated the leaders of the Peasants' Revolt after the killing of Wat Tyler. But he could not then continue the authority of the moment, and his council, by rescinding the pardons he had granted and hanging the leaders of the rebellion, permanently slurred Richard's good faith.

Throughout his reign Richard showed no interest in wars or foreign adventures. Yet he lived amid almost continual strife, much of it reflecting the personal ambition and political rigidity of his three powerful uncles, the dukes of Lancaster, York and Gloucester. Lancaster (John of Gaunt) had schemes for the acquisition of the throne, and he passed this design on to his son Henry of Bolingbroke, then Earl of Derby. This almost permanent aristocratic opposition to the reigning king was crystallized, for public show, around the irritants of Richard's tendency to autocracy and the foreign atmosphere

Right *Richard II, grandson of Edward III and known as Richard of Bordeaux, at his coronation.*

Bottom *Richard II rides out to meet his subjects – from a manuscript of Froissart's Chronicles.*

Below *A contemporary impression of the murder of the Archbishop of Canterbury by supporters of Wat Tyler.*

of his court which resulted from Queen Anne's origin in Bohemia, in the Holy Roman Empire. 'Foreign' then implied 'not French'; but it was Richard's regency council who had ordained Richard's marriage to Anne, precisely because they wanted a Central European ally *against* France. Richard and Anne, brought together for stark reasons of state, became devoted to each other through their 12 years of marriage, but they had no children. There is no known ground at all for the suggestion of homosexuality in Richard which has been made because of his character as a dandy and an aesthete.

Autocracy was certainly his aim, and Parliament was used with some skill to defeat it. By the time he was 19, Richard was attempting to rule through favourites whom he had appointed to his household, and through the silent menace to the constitution represented by that household itself, which numbered 10,000 and was inevitably an expensive burden on national finance. But Parliament, led by the dissident dukes and their associates, the influential Earls of Warwick, Arundel and Nottingham, gave a clear hint at an early stage that kings could be deposed for arbitrary non cooperation. And the unruly lords took up arms, drove some of Richard's appointed officials into exile and captured others who were subsequently executed. The confrontation was undisguised.

Richard waited for over a year, and in a carefully prepared *coup d'état* resumed personal government. Once it was accepted, he diplomatically renewed friendship and even partnership with the aristocratic opposition. But after the great shock of the death of Queen Anne in 1394, and perhaps through the loss of her modifying influence, his actions pointed more sharply towards extreme absolutism and exaggerated personal extravagance. In the ensuing unrest the six leaders of the dissident peers were split into two groups by Richard. The king temporarily 'bought' John of Gaunt by legitimizing the children of John's long liaison with Katherine Swynford. This affair had been going on for such a time, through the lifetime of his two wives, that the children of the union were almost as old as John's heir, Henry of Bolingbroke. The consequences of this act of legitimization, which was carelessly done to buy a favour, were to govern the succession to the English throne. The four children of the union, who were surnamed Beaufort, advanced high in prestige. One became a Cardinal, one Earl of Somerset, one Duke of Exeter, and the daughter married the Earl of Westmoreland. The daughter of John Beaufort, Earl of Somerset, was the mother of King Henry VII.

Richard's gesture towards John of Gaunt had pleased John's son, Henry Earl of Derby, who did not consider his claim to the throne menaced by the action. Derby then influenced the Earl of Nottingham not to oppose the king for the moment. There remained the Duke of Gloucester and the Earls of Arundel and Warwick. Richard arrested these three lords. Henry Earl of Derby personally accused the Earl of Arundel

of treachery, then officially, as High Steward, passed sentence of death on him, and the execution took place immediately. Of the others, Warwick was exiled and Richard's uncle, the Duke of Gloucester, was sent to Calais where he died in prison, reputedly murdered. Derby and Nottingham were promptly created Dukes of Hereford and Norfolk. Derby then accused of treason the only lord remaining among the prime conspirators (barring his father) – the newly created Duke of Norfolk. Richard decreed that the accusation should be settled through ordeal by battle, trial by single combat. A joust to the death was set up at Coventry before an immense concourse of people. But, as the two contestants were cantering into the charge, Richard peremptorily cancelled the fight and

banished both Dukes from England.

Soon after Henry left the country, his father John of Gaunt died. Richard deprived the heir of his inheritance. Henry seized the opportunity of Richard's absence in Ireland to land in Yorkshire, at Ravenspur 'to claim his father's duchy'. Having reached the lands of Lancaster, he went farther, captured Richard, and brought him to the Tower of London. On September 29, 1399 Richard formally abdicated the throne before a mixed committee of peers and commoners, and the court officials broke their staves of office. On September 30, at a full meeting of Parliament in Westminster Hall, Henry of Lancaster rose from his place on the dukes' bench and strode forward towards the empty throne crying 'I challenge (claim) this kingdom and

crown'. In spite of a tumultuous acclamation in London, he was soon aware that he was opposed in some quarters as a usurper. He provoked his enemies into conspiracy, caught them and killed them. He felt finally at peace when it was reported to him that Richard of Bordeaux was dead in prison.

Henry IV
1399-1413

Known as Henry of Bolingbroke

Born at Bolingbroke, Lincolnshire, on April 3, 1367.
Succeeded as King of England and Lord of Ireland on September 30, 1399

Left *The marriage of Richard II and Isabella of France.*

Below *Richard II abdicates, on September 29, 1399, after 22 years.*

aged 32.

Cousin of his predecessor Richard, both being grandsons of King Edward III. Henry was the sixth child and eldest surviving son of John of Gaunt and Blanche (Plantagenet) of Lancaster. Allowing for strict primogeniture and admitting succession through the female line, he was strictly a usurper because of the prior claim to the throne of Edmund Mortimer, fifth Earl of March, the son of Roger Mortimer, fourth Earl, who was Richard's and Henry's second cousin but was a step higher in priority than Henry: for Roger was the grandson of Lionel of Antwerp, John of Gaunt's elder brother, through Lionel's daughter Philippa, who married Edmund Mortimer, third Earl of March (the great-grandson of that Roger Mortimer, first Earl of March, the executed lover of the mother of Edward III – and thus time brought in its revenges. The roundabout turned again when the great-grandsons of Roger, fourth Earl took the throne as Edward IV and Richard III). Richard II had nominated Roger

fourth Earl, as his heir. When Roger, as Viceroy in Ireland, was killed in a skirmish Richard II resolutely went to Ireland to reimpose order. It was during this fortuitous opportunity of Richard's absence in Ireland that the exiled Henry reentered England and emerged as king.

Married 1. probably in 1385 when he was 18, Mary Bohun, co-heiress with her sister Eleanor (who married Henry's uncle Thomas, Duke of Gloucester) of Humphrey de Bohun, Earl of Hereford. Mary was a descendant of King Henry III and called herself Plantagenet. She died in 1394. 2. in 1397 when he was 30 and the bride was 27, Joan of Navarre, daughter of King Charles II of Navarre. She survived him and died in 1437.
Children all of Mary, a son who died in infancy, HENRY, Thomas, John, Humphrey, Blanche, Philippa.
Died in the Jerusalem Chamber of the Abbot's house at Westminster, of heart disease after five years' misery from an aggravated skin complaint, on March 20, 1413, aged 45, having reigned

13 years. Buried in Canterbury Cathedral.

Profile stocky build, red hair worn short, with a long serpentine moustache and a short forked beard. Physically energetic, and a first-rate swordsman. Sharp-tongued and with some wit, ambitious and politically double-dealing, yet with his thinking and conscience always coloured by an intensively religious upbringing.

꙳꙳꙳꙳꙳꙳꙳꙳꙳꙳꙳꙳꙳꙳

Henry was the first king since the Conqueror who was born in England of English parents. But he scarcely knew his mother, who died when he was two, and rarely met his father until he was nine, when John of Gaunt came home from foreign administration and fighting to take over the government from his dying brother Edward III. By the age of 20 Henry, as Earl of Derby and a confidant of his father's ambition for power, was one of the five Lords Appellant who militarily defeated Richard's ruling clique and deprived the king of absolute sovereignty. Advised by his father to show neutrality, and later friendship, towards King Richard, he spent three adventurous years in Europe and then returned to political influence, to see his former confederates removed one by one until only the newly-created Duke of Norfolk was left. Norfolk told Henry, whom he considered his oldest friend in statesmanship, that Richard was not to be trusted. An involved situation then developed. Henry knew that Norfolk was right: if Richard had killed or exiled four of the six who stood between him and autocracy, why should he spare the other two? But, since Richard worked through conspiracy – even getting Norfolk to kill Richard's uncle Gloucester – how could Henry know that he was not being trapped by Richard through conniving at a treason suggested by Norfolk as Richard's *agent provocateur*? The safest action was to abandon friendship and demonstrate loyalty by denouncing Norfolk, and Henry did so. But, on the occasion of the staged duel to the death between Henry and Norfolk at Coventry, Richard suddenly realised that Henry had enormous popularity with the huge crowd of spectators who reflected the feelings of the populace at large. If Henry won the fight, he could expect to

be possibly more influential than the king, and there would be no rival who could be used to put him down. Richard therefore impulsively banned the duel at the last moment and exiled both contestants.

John of Gaunt, Duke of Lancaster, then died. Henry, in exile near Paris, heard that Richard had confiscated all the Lancaster estates and lengthened Henry's banishment to a life sentence. Richard went to Ireland, for a valid military reason but with an ill-judged sense of survival. When Henry landed in Yorkshire he was joined by the Duke of York, the Regent whom Richard had appointed for England and the only survivor of those four politically formidable brothers, the Black Prince, Lionel Duke of Clarence, John Duke of Lancaster and Edmund Duke of York. Against this combination, and an army of 100,000 men, Richard had no hope. All that Henry had to carry through, to tidy the operation after his enthronement, was to kill off Richard's elder half-brothers (Richard's mother, the Fair Maid of Kent, had sons from a marriage previous to her union with the Black Prince), and finally Richard himself.

Henry, always over-anxious about his 'usurpation' of the throne from the young Earl of March (whom he imprisoned at Windsor through the whole length of his reign), ostentatiously maintained that he owed his position to the decision of Parliament – and the three estates of Parliament pressed home the advantage by demanding their pounds of flesh. The Commons obtained promises of freedom of speech in return for voting money. The Church insisted on a heresy-hunt which Richard had always resisted, and the first heretics were burned at the stake in Henry's reign. The Lords Temporal wanted power and plunder, which Henry half-granted by sanctioning operations in France and against the Welsh and the Scots, which later the belligerent lords converted into revolts against Henry himself. In the North Marches particularly, the Earl of Northumberland, his son Hotspur, and Archbishop Scrope of York waged open rebellion. Henry finally put this down by battle and by the execution of the Archbishop, later getting absolution from the Pope for the sacrilege. For the last half of his term Henry was ill with heart disease. He died miserably after a personally wretched reign, yet he had ruled in difficult times with fair statesmanship, and was in advance of his time as a constitutional monarch.

Left *An engraving of Henry IV and his second wife, Joan of Navarre.*

Right *A scene from the coronation of Henry of Bolingbroke, when he was crowned as Henry IV.*

Below *This impression of the Battle of Shrewsbury comes from a nineteenth century history of England.*

Henry V
1413-1422

Known as Henry of Monmouth

Born at Monmouth on August 9, 1387. **Succeeded** as King of England and Lord of Ireland on March 20, 1413 aged 25. In 1420 was accepted as Regent of France and successor to the French throne.

Eldest surviving son of his predecessor Henry, his elder brother having died in babyhood.

Married on June 2, 1420, when he was 32 and the bride was 19, Catherine of Valois, daughter of King Charles VI of France. She survived him, and later married – secretly, and according to some authorities dubiously – Sir Owen Tudor, who was executed by Yorkists during the Wars of the Roses. She died in 1437, as a nun in Bermondsey Abbey. **Child** HENRY.

Died of dysentery at Paris on August 31, 1422, aged 35 having reigned nine years. Buried in Westminster Abbey.

Profile very tall (6ft 3in), slim, with dark hair cropped in a ring above the ears, clean-shaven and with a shaven neck, displaying under a ruddy complexion a lean face with a prominently pointed nose. According to his mood, his eyes flashed 'from the mildness of a dove's to the brilliance of a lion's'. He was a dandy, but not a rake, in his youth and was a professional soldier from the time of his teens. His enthusiasms were for hunting and music. He had a reputation for compassion towards the underdog in peacetime, but was totally ruthless in war, and in conformist religion.

❦❦❦❦❦❦❦❦❦❦❦❦❦

As a boy, Henry had been kindly treated by Richard II in spite of his father's turbulent behaviour, and as king, Henry belatedly observed Richard's last wishes and brought his body to be reinterred with his devoted wife. He was aged 12 when his father succeeded, and he swore that what Bolingbroke had gained by the sword should be kept by the son's sword if necessary. But, apart from one rising in favour of the Earl of March (whom he had released from imprisonment), there

was little serious opposition and the military energy of the nobles was directed into war against France. When the war was seen to be successful, he had the populace behind him throughout his short reign, and as an absentee king found loyal delegates in government.

Henry revived Edward III's claim to the French throne, and sailed in August 1415 to besiege Harfleur. When the town fell, he challenged the Dauphin of France to personal combat, the prize being the territories of Normandy, Anjou, Maine and Touraine and Henry's marriage to the Dauphin's sister Catherine. The one-sided offer was ignored. Henry marched towards Calais,

and met the French army at Agincourt, a battle which was later treated by Shakespeare with notable accuracy, even in the set speeches, although the dramatist's previous creation of a wild Prince Hal and an invented Falstaff was a libel totally exonerated by its genius.

After a lapse of two years of diplomacy and conspiracy, Henry again invaded France in 1417 and conquered all Normandy. But he irreparably stained his character by refusing to let pass through his lines 12,000 non-combatants who had been expelled from Rouen as counter-productive during a siege, and he watched them die of starvation in the town ditch during the six-months siege. After continuing the campaign

southwards for two more years, Henry exacted a treaty which recognized him as Regent of France, as the next King of France (instead of the Dauphin), and as the bridegroom of the French king's daughter Catherine. Under these conditions he married Catherine and spent Christmas in Paris with the King of France. After a brief return to England to crown and deposit his queen, he again left for France to counter the recalcitrant Dauphin. Christmas in Paris that year was enlivened by news of the birth at Windsor of his son and heir. But with the spring, the campaign against the Dauphin was resumed, and Henry, after a long resistance, capitulated to the common soldier's disease of dysentery. In the large, Grecian, sense of the word, this man had been a hero.

Opposite below *A classic portrait of King Henry V.*

Top left *Henry V wooing Catherine of France, whom he later married.*

Below *Henry V's tilting helm, saddle and inner face of his shield.*

Overleaf *The Battle of Agincourt, in 1415, was a personal triumph for Henry V and his English archers.*

Henry VI
1422-1461,
1470-1471

Born in Windsor Castle on December 6, 1421.

Succeeded as King of England and Lord of Ireland on August 31, 1422 aged eight months, as King of France in October 1422 aged ten months.

Only son of his predecessor Henry.

Married at Winchester in May 1444, when he was 22 and the bride was 14, Margaret of Anjou, daughter of René, titular King of Sicily, Duke of Lorraine and Count of Provence. (He was called 'René the Good', but also, since he claimed many titles but had little land, though much culture, 'the King of the Troubadors'). Margaret survived Henry and died in poverty in 1482.

Child Edward.

Died murdered in the Tower of London on May 21, 1471, aged 50, having reigned, excluding intervals as a refugee and prisoner, 40 years; and having reigned as recognized King of France for 13 years. Buried first at Chertsey Abbey, later at Windsor, and possibly later reinterred at Westminster.

Profile in maturity, tall but not strong, with brown curly hair, short-cut over his ears and shaven at the neck, on a small head, exposing a long, clean-shaven face, not handsome. He always dressed himself inconspicuously in black, with a simple hooded jacket and a farmer's round-toed boots, all worn over a hair-shirt next to the skin. He was the most truly humble and genuinely Christian of all English kings, though not without prudery, and he was a rare practising pacifist. Mentally, he succumbed for a period, under the severe stress of civil war, to a hereditary melancholia which removed him from the practical world. He came out of this to renew his pursuit of excellence – in education, in architecture, and in general culture – with the detailed construction of Eton College and King's College, Cambridge. As a king, in an age of ruthlessness which far exceeded the manners of preceding times, he was a tragic misfit.

ಌಌಌಌಌಌಌ

Left *Portrait of Henry VI, who succeeded to the throne at the age of ten months. He reigned 40 years.*

Above *King's College, Cambridge was founded by Henry VI, who showed himself devoted to architecture.*

Right *Richard Neville, known as Warwick the Kingmaker, a powerful Lancastrian supporter, visits Henry in the Tower.*

Henry V had been recognized by formal treaty as heir to the kingdom of France, and would have occupied that throne himself if he had lived two months longer. On the death of Charles VI of France in October 1422, Henry VI, as son of Henry and grandson of Charles, succeeded as legitimate King of France at the age of ten months. The boy king was crowned in Westminster Abbey on November 6, 1429, and in Notre Dame, Paris, on December 16, 1431. Henry's uncle, brother of Queen Catherine, had been proclaimed as King Charles VII of France in Bourges at the same time that Henry was proclaimed King of France in Paris. After the efforts of Joan of Arc, Charles was crowned in Reims in July 1429. As a boy of eight, Henry was present at Joan's trial in Rouen the following year. The Duke of Burgundy renounced recognition of Henry as King of France in 1435, and this marks the *de facto* end of Henry's reign over France. For the rest of his life his temporal preoccupation concerned his tenure of the throne of England, which was under pressure.

Henry was always dominated by strong-minded psychological bullies. They were, at first, his immediate heirs, his uncles, the brothers of Henry V, John Duke of Bedford and Humphrey Duke

Above *The wedding of Henry VI in 1444. His bride was the strong willed Margaret of Anjou. Her influence added to the stress of ambitious factions surrounding Henry.*

Opposite below *A painting by H. A. Payne shows Yorkists and Lancastrians plucking the opposing symbols of a white and red rose.*

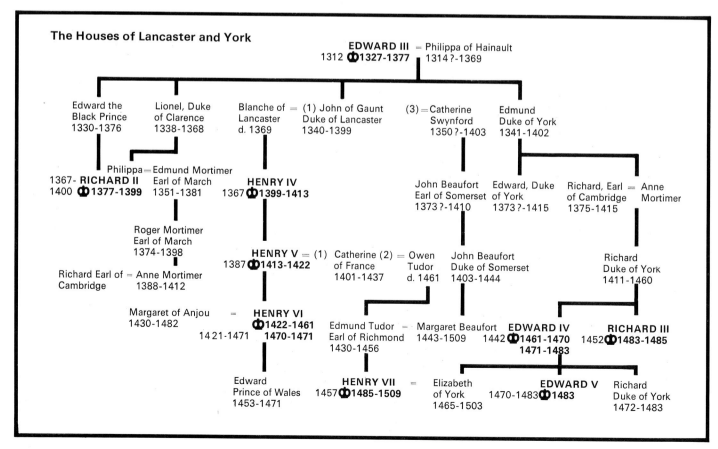

The Houses of Lancaster and York

of Gloucester, and his second cousin Richard Duke of York. These were, in the main, at permanent odds with his other cousins, the Beauforts, the tardily legitimized descendants of John of Gaunt by his union with Katherine Swynford. They and their children, apart from the grave statesman Henry, Cardinal Beaufort, Bishop of Winchester, are a remarkable witness to the ferocity of the Wars of the Roses if only by the manner in which they met their deaths: Edmund, Duke of Somerset, killed at St Albans 1455; Henry, Duke of Somerset, executed 1464; Edmund, Duke of Somerset, executed 1471. These were Lancastrians, yet one branch of the Beauforts was Yorkist except for the ambitiously ambivalent Richard Neville, Warwick the King-Maker. Their fate was little different: Joan Beaufort's son, Richard Neville, and son-in-law, Richard Duke of York, both executed 1460; her grandson, Richard Neville (Warwick the King-Maker), killed at Barnet 1471. The last, and perhaps the most fear-

some, force governing Henry VI was his wife Margaret of Anjou.

The political struggle amongst these personalities first polarized into a battle. It was between Richard Duke of York, heir presumptive to the throne for six years until Queen Margaret bore a child, and the first Somerset. Somerset himself, a descendant of John of Gaunt, Duke of Lancaster, emphasized the legitimists' nickname of Lancastrians. Somerset was killed in battle with York. York allied himself and his son, Edward Earl of March, with the powerful Nevilles, but was later executed by Queen Margaret's orders after being captured at the battle of Tewkesbury. Edward Earl of March, now Duke of York, then proclaimed himself king and maintained his position by force.

King Henry VI had married Margaret of Anjou in 1444 as a diplomatic action to seal a truce with France. Six years later, during her first and only pregnancy, the king had a paralytic stroke which made him mentally incapable. After some months he recovered, but when

he was forcibly involved in the battle of St. Albans, he was wounded by an arrow through the neck, and relapsed into imbecility. The king's pacifist principles usually prevented him from fighting, but with great courage, he often attended many of the battles of this fierce war. During a year of impotence, Queen Margaret channelled power into her own hands for the sake of her infant son. But, though she won three battles in 1460, she was forced by Edward Duke of York, now calling himself King Edward IV, to retreat with Henry VI and the Prince of Wales to Scotland, and thence independently to France while Henry remained in the north.

In 1465 Henry was captured, and imprisoned by Edward in the Tower of London. After five years Warwick the King-Maker quarrelled with Edward IV and conspired with Queen Margaret and King Louis XI of France to restore Henry to the throne. The plan succeeded, but within six months Edward IV reinvaded England with an army of Burgundians, and at the battle of Barnet killed Warwick and recaptured Henry. A month later Henry's son, Edward Prince of Wales, accompanied another invasion of England with his mother the queen, and was killed at the age of 17 in (or more probably executed after) the battle of Tewkesbury. Within another month King Henry VI was murdered in the Tower of London, possibly on the orders of Richard Duke of Gloucester, the brother of King Edward IV, and a future king.

Edward IV
1461-1470, 1471-1483

Born at Rouen on April 28, 1442.
Claimed the Crown of England and Ireland and was accepted by proclamation on March 5, 1461 at the age of 18. He abandoned the throne to Henry VI by fleeing to Flanders in September 1470. He succeeded without open dispute to the throne when King Henry VI died on May 21, 1471.
Third cousin of his predecessor Henry, both being great-great-grandsons of King Edward III. (See the note on

Dynasties and Usurpers, below).

Marriage After possibly entering into a binding contract of marriage with Lady Eleanor Butler, reputedly to overcome her objections to being seduced, Edward secretly married, on May 1, 1464, when he was 22 and the bride was 27, the widowed Dame Elizabeth Grey, daughter of Richard Woodville, Earl Rivers. She survived him and died as a nun in Bermondsey Abbey in 1492.

Children Elizabeth of York (Henry VII's future Queen), Mary, Cicely, EDWARD, Margaret, Richard, George, Anne, Catherine, Bridget.

Mistresses among many, Jane Shore, Elizabeth Lacy.

Bastards among many, Arthur Plantagenet, Lord de Lisle and Elizabeth Lumley, ancestor of the Earls of Scarborough, both by Elizabeth Lacy.

Died at Westminster, of a fever following over-eating, on April 9, 1483, aged 40, having reigned 22 years. Buried in St George's Chapel, Windsor, which he had rebuilt to rival King Henry VI's Eton College Chapel.

Profile 6ft tall, at first outstandingly handsome, clean-shaven with straight brown hair worn long. Always interested in dress and a gay social life, dancing and banqueting. His dissolute sexual practices diseased him early, and with his gluttony he became prematurely fat, and died of a surfeit. He was a sound practical, and ruthless, soldier and a competent financial manager. His interest in the dissemination of knowledge made him more than the titular patron of William Caxton, the printer.

🙚🙚🙚🙚🙚🙚🙚🙚🙚🙚🙚

A note on Dynasties and Usurpers
The following analysis sets down as simply as possible the hereditary situation which was exploited both by Lancastrians and Yorkists, and resolved by the Tudors. Henry VI and Edward IV were both great-great-grandsons of Edward III. Henry was the great-grandson of John of Gaunt, Duke of Lancaster, who was an elder brother of Edmund of Langley, Duke of York, who was Edward IV's great grandfather. But, if succession through the female line is admitted, Edward had a stronger claim to seniority than Henry, though he and his father did not publish it until an opportune moment in 1460. Edward's grandmother, Anne Mortimer, was a descendant of Edward III through that king's second surviving son, Lionel

Below The coronation of Edward IV at Westminster in 1461.

Right *A window from Canterbury Cathedral portraying Edward's family.*

Ciwardus dei gracia Lex Anglie et fraucie et dominus hibernie

Regina Elizabetha consors Edwardi dei gracia Lepis

of Antwerp, Duke of Clarence, who was older than both Lancaster and York and junior only to the Black Prince, the father of Richard II. Clarence's line was continued through the marriage of his only child, Philippa, to Edmund Mortimer, third Earl of March. Their son Roger was declared heir to the throne by Richard II, but died before Richard.

When the Lancastrian Henry IV took the throne from Richard and from the son of Roger Mortimer, that act was usurpation. This son of Roger – Edmund Mortimer, fifth Earl of March – although imprisoned throughout the reign of Henry IV, outlived Henry IV and Henry V, but had no issue. The family claim to the throne was taken up by descendants of Edmund's sister Anne Mortimer, a great-great-granddaughter of Edward III who married Richard Earl of Cambridge, a grandson of Edward III. Their grandson was Edward IV, who was also (though he based no claim on the connection) great-great-grandson to Edward III through his mother Cicely Neville, Countess of Northumberland, daughter of Joan Beaufort who was daughter of John of Gaunt.

Until the birth of Edward Prince of Wales in 1453, Edward IV's father Richard, Duke of York had been the accepted heir to Henry VI relying only on descent from Edward III in the male line, through John of Gaunt's younger brother, Edmund Duke of York. This acceptance passed over the claims of the Beaufort family by excluding from the succession the legitimatized children of Katherine Swynford and John of Gaunt, Duke of Lancaster, the senior brother of York. But it was this excluded line which was very soon to take over the crown for more than a century, with the Tudor dynasty.

Edward's grandfather, Richard Earl of Cambridge, had been executed by Henry V for rebellion in support of the claim to the throne of the young Earl of March. Edward's father, Richard Duke of York, killed during or executed after the battle of Wakefield when claiming the throne from Henry VI, had his head set on the walls of York city garlanded with a paper crown. At the age of 18, therefore, Edward, as the next Duke of York, was a pretender to the throne. Within three months of his father's death he was proclaimed king.

Within three months more he had confirmed his claim in battle, and was crowned. There were still four years of fighting before Henry VI was captured and confined in the Tower of London. But before this event Edward had had to give up soldiering because of the condition of his health, brought on by sexual excesses. He had also contracted a clandestine marriage with Elizabeth Grey, née Woodville. The reason for this marriage – performed at dawn with only four witnesses, and not revealed until five months later – seems to be the simple fact that Elizabeth would not yield herself as a concubine. It was the same motive as existed for Edward's reputed previous betrothal to Eleanor Butler. At least it can be said that Edward was one of the rare English monarchs who married for the passion of love. And the reason why it was kept secret for as long as possible was that it destroyed the opportunity to negotiate a politically important dynastic marriage between Edward and a foreign princess which was being actively pursued by his powerful cousin Richard Neville, Earl of Warwick and Salisbury.

Warwick, with his many influential Neville relations in the north, and in alliance with Edward's younger brother

Below Contemporary view of the Battle of Barnet, 1471.

Right A woodcut from Caxton's printed edition of The Canterbury Tales.

George, Duke of Clarence, had for long occupied the commanding heights of political power, after having been instrumental in securing the throne for Edward and maintaining him there for the first four years. Edward now began to create a counter-clique. He ennobled useful members of his wife's family, gave them office at Court, and married her five sisters within a year into the families of peers whose estates lay mainly in the south. By 1469 the Nevilles were in revolt in the north, and Warwick and Clarence occupied the strategic strongpoint of Calais. Eventually Warwick and Clarence joined Queen Margaret, then living in exile in Paris, and invaded England. Edward, with no support except the company of his 18-year-old brother Richard, Duke of Gloucester, fled to Flanders. Warwick reappointed Henry VI as king, and ruled in his name.

In March 1471 Edward landed with 2000 men at Ravenspur, where Henry IV had returned from exile to win the throne, and Clarence deserted Warwick to join him. After Edward's despatch of Warwick at the battle of Barnet, and his victory over Queen Margaret at Tewkesbury, it was King Edward's brothers Clarence and Gloucester, and Queen Elizabeth's son Thomas Grey, Marquis of Dorset, who murdered the Prince of Wales, son of Henry and Margaret, according to the circumstantial account which says the boy was not killed in the battle. Whether, almost immediately, Gloucester himself murdered Henry VI is a matter of insoluble controversy. Later, King Edward, encouraged by Richard of Gloucester, suspected Clarence of plotting fresh treason, and, after sentencing him to death, had him drowned in a butt of Malmsey wine in the Tower of London. The toll of sovereignty through assassination, so characteristic of Edward's time, was to be continued against his immediate family after his death.

Edward IV ruled throughout his reign as a despot. He rarely summoned a Parliament, and then only to announce a war, for which they voted money. Having obtained the money, he called off the war. On one occasion he led an expedition into France and allowed himself to be bought off by King Louis XI at a price of 75,000 gold crowns down and a regular annuity of 20,000 more. This was mere pocket money compared with his personal income, drawn from his huge hereditary estates and the land he confiscated from defeated Lancastrians, which together made him proprietor of one-fifth of the area of England. Owning so much land, and therefore so many sheep, he held a vested interest in the English wool trade, which he guided into great prosperity, both to his personal gain and to the advantage of the country. Indeed, although he lived in opulence, he did plough back most of his profits into the administration and economy of the country. There was no distinction then between the King's Privy Purse, a Civil List, and the transactions of his Treasury. The king ran the country out of his own budget. It was no small tribute to his skill, and greatly to his people's economic benefit, that he was the first king of England for many centuries who died free of debt.

Edward V
1483

Born in the Abbot's house in Westminster on November 2, 1470.
Succeeded as King of England and Lord of Ireland on April 9, 1483, aged 12. Deposed on June 25, 1483, having reigned 11 weeks.
Eldest son of his predecessor Edward.
Died in the Tower of London by being smothered, in late August 1483, aged 12. Buried in the Tower, and reinterred

𝕻rologue

Of ecſe of þem ſo as it ſemed me
And whyche they were and of what degre
And in what aray eſe they weryn ynne
And at a knyght þenne I wyl begynne

Knyght þer was a worthy man
That fro þe tyme þat he firſt began
To ryden out / he loued chyualrye
Trouthe & honour fredom and curteſye

two centuries later in Westminster Abbey.

🙜🙜🙜🙜🙜🙜🙜🙜🙜🙜🙜

Edward was born, six years after his parents' marriage although Queen Elizabeth had had other sons by her first marriage. His father had fled to Flanders in 1470, when the queen took sanctuary in Westminster Abbey. He was made Prince of Wales after the murder of the son of Henry VI. He had been carefully and discreetly trained for his future office, and soon after his father's death he set off from Ludlow in the care of his half-brother and his uncle – his relations on his mother's side – to take his place formally in Westminster. Richard Earl of Gloucester, who had been named Protector of the Kingdom, arrested the boy's escort en route, alleging conspiracy, and personally conducted the young king to London. Queen Elizabeth took sanctuary with her younger son, Richard Duke of York, once again in Westminster Abbey. Richard, as Protector, lodged King Edward V in the Tower of London, and called a council there on June 13, 1483 to decide the details of the coronation. At this meeting, as one of the members of the council described it, Richard theatrically provoked an atmosphere of the heavy doom of treason, accused Queen Elizabeth of witchcraft and the Chamberlain, William Lord Hastings, of treachery, and declared that he would not eat dinner until Hastings' head was severed from his body – which was immediately done on Tower Green.

Hastings had been the fourth member of the noble gang, including Grey, Clarence and Gloucester, who had stabbed the last Prince of Wales to death. It is a sign of the dramatic unpredictability of the times. Richard then confined other members of the council in the Tower, and displayed himself to the citizens of London in beaten-up armour, saying that he had barely escaped assassination. He promptly murdered Edward's maternal rela-

Above *The Tower of London where the young brothers were suffocated.*

Below right *Edward V was murdered by order of his uncle, Richard, before his coronation could take place.*

Above *The Princes in the Tower portrayed by the artist Millais.*

Below *Before going to London, the brothers stayed at Ludlow Castle.*

tives whom he had already arrested on the way to London. He next used the Archbishop of Canterbury to persuade Queen Elizabeth to release the Duke of York from sanctuary into the company of his brother in the Tower of London. He then started a propaganda campaign to assert that the new king and the Duke of York were bastards, because of a reputed earlier betrothal of Edward IV to Lady Eleanor Butler, an allegation which is credible, and according to the customs of the time substantial, for which there is now no reliable evidence.

In any case, the illegitimacy of the present king would admit the heirs of Edward IV's next younger brother, senior to Gloucester, George Duke of Clarence. Richard putatively disposed of them by declaring that since Clarence had been attainted for treason, Clarence's children were *personae non gratae*. Finding little popular response, Richard manipulated a deputation from Parliament to request him to accept the crown, and on June 25, 1483 he graciously submitted. Eleven days later he was crowned. He went to the West Country to display himself and arouse enthus-

iasm, and left orders for King Edward V and his brother to be killed in the Tower. When these orders were disobeyed, he sent Sir James Tyrell to the Tower with a commission to take over command of the fortress for one night. During this night the 'Princes in the Tower' were suffocated.

Richard III
1483-1485

Known as Richard Crookback

Born on October 2, 1452 at Fotheringay Castle, Northamptonshire.
Acceded 'by request of Parliament' as King of England and Lord of Ireland on June 25, 1483 at the age of 30.
Uncle of his predecessor Edward V and younger brother of Edward IV.
Married in 1473, when he was aged 20 and the bride 15, Anne Neville, daughter of his cousin Richard Earl of Warwick (the King-maker) and widow (when she was 13) of Henry VI's heir, Edward

Prince of Wales, whom Richard had gang-murdered after the battle of Tewkesbury. She died wretchedly in 1485.

Child Edward, who died as newly-created Prince of Wales in 1484.

Bastards Among others, Richard Plantagenet, master-builder, and John of Gloucester, Governor of Guisnes.

Died in battle near Market Bosworth, Leicestershire on August 22, 1485, having reigned two years. Buried ignominiously in the Grey Friars' Abbey, Leicester where Henry VII later provided a more ornate tomb.

Profile Said to have been attractive in youth, but never after adolescence. Medium height, clean-shaven with long bobbed reddish-brown hair, having a small pale face and thin lips. Nervous in his habits, often easing his dagger in and out of its sheath. He was a very good general, and his courage and skill in individual combat compensated for the physical disability of having his right shoulder hunched high and his left arm slightly withered – features which the artist has skilfully treated in the painting now in the National Portrait Gallery.

꙳꙳꙳꙳꙳꙳꙳꙳꙳꙳꙳꙳꙳

History has been said to be propaganda written by the victors. All the accounts of the reign of Richard III, the last of a royal line which had been established for three centuries, were written for the consumption of the victorious Tudors. Even the most plausible contemporary chronicle was set down by Sir Thomas More from conversations with Archbishop Morton held when Morton was over 70 and More about 16 years old. Admittedly, this was within six years of Richard's death, but the narrator was a man who had served on the councils of Edward IV, Edward V, Richard III and Henry VII, and had candidly plotted to oust Richard. However, it is really quite irrelevant to a report on the progress of England whether Richard was the ogre whom Holinshed and Shakespeare presented a century later, or the comparatively whitewashed gentleman' whom some modern historians are now unveiling. As a king, Richard was a cipher. He changed nothing in England except by the manner in which he was overthrown and replaced. The heavy drama of his life was played out principally during the reigns of other

RICARDVS · III · ANG · REX ·

monarchs, and has already been told.

Throughout his short reign Richard was keenly aware of the plotting which was being pursued against him. He knew the identity of the man who, it was planned, should succeed him and the identity of his proposed bride. The man was Henry Tudor, Earl of Richmond, a nominal Lancastrian through his descent from John of Gaunt. The bride was to be Elizabeth of York, the eldest daughter of Edward IV and Elizabeth Woodville, and the marriage was planned as a union of the two heirs of the Red and White Rose factions.

Henry had been resident in France for 12 years, on the advice of King Henry VI, who knew too well the danger hovering over even distant heirs to the throne. He attempted a premature invasion in October 1483, within four months of Richard's accession. But he could not slip past the royal navy, and merely presented Richard with the opportunity to identify Henry's principal supporters within England and chop off their heads. Richard also set a virtual siege-force round Westminster Abbey, where Elizabeth of York was in sanctuary, so that she could not escape to be married. In the next year Richard's only son, Edward Prince of Wales, died. There was no heir of his blood. Richard's wife, Anne, was sickly, and the king immediately began to pay elaborate court to his niece, Elizabeth of York, intending that she should marry him although he had killed her two brothers after declaring them, and her, to be illegitimate. But even the cowed citizens of London could not stomach this charade, and Richard withdrew.

He spent a feverish year preparing for the inevitable invasion, which was finally effected on August 7, 1485 at Milford Haven. Henry marched eastwards through Wales, which he regarded as his homeland, gathering support with every stride. Richard met him at Bosworth Field, near Leicester. Richard had an army superior in numbers but very deficient in morale. In the ensuing two-hour battle Richard, a superb fighter, might well have killed Henry, who was not. But Henry's bodyguard gave him cover during one bout of single combat, and finally cut Richard down. The gold coronet which the king had worn over his helmet had been hacked off in the *melée*, and fell into a bush. Symbolically Lord Stanley, who with many nobles in the vicinity of the battle had kept his troops out of the fight, placed the crown on the head of Henry Tudor. It was the end of an ugly era.

The Rulers of Wales

King Henry VII, born in Pembroke, had marched 200 miles into battle beneath the standard of the Red Dragon of Wales, and he was the first English monarch to incorporate that emblem into the Royal Standard. It is fitting that, at this point, the tally of the rulers of Wales should be recounted. The Celts, or Britons, were Christians by the year 200 A.D., and never abandoned this formal faith nor their ancient tribal ways when they were driven by the Anglo-Saxon invaders into Cornwall, Cumberland and Wales. In Wales the rulers (who in this account will mainly be referred to as 'lords' for convenience) were recognized as kings, princes or chieftains according to the size of their territory, but were mutually independent. None were vassals to any other lord. Sometimes a powerful leader would consolidate the Welsh into unity. But, all too swiftly, any potential national cohesion fell apart, mainly because the belligerent Welsh lords were fighting each other for self-aggrandizement with little sense of nationhood.

Gradually, however, three areas began to be recognized as the hotbeds of mature development, even if they still seethed with the expression of lesser local loyalties and rivalries. They were the north, the south and the east, Gwynedd, Deheubarth and Powys. Deheubarth did not include Morgannwg (Glamorgan) in the south, but did sometimes comprise Ceredigion (modern Cardiganshire) in the west. Powys (roughly from the river Dee to the river Wye) had temporarily become absorbed into Gwynedd by the middle of the ninth century when this chronicle begins. This came about under the rule of MERFYN FRYCH 825–844 (Merfyn the Freckled), the lord of Gwynedd who married the daughter of the lord of Powys, and whose son

Above *View across the Usk at Abergavenny and its castle.*

Below *Rhodri Mawr, first after Cadwallon to unite Wales.*

RHODRI MAWR 844–878 (Rhodri the Great) was the first, after the old Cadwallon, to unite most of the land of Wales. He did this through military skill and political expediency. His spirited resistance against Norse invasions inspired many other lords to unite to keep the Norsemen out of Wales; and he married Angharad, the daughter of the lord of Greater Ceredigion. He was not a storybook conqueror, always successful. In 876 he had to flee to Ireland to escape the menace of the Northmen, and in 878 he was killed in battle with the English. Rhodri left six sons and, according to ancient (and ill-starred) Welsh custom, they divided the 'kingdom' of Wales between them. Those who emerged with power were Anarawd in Gwynedd and Cadell in Ceredigion.

ANARAWD 878–916 first made an alliance with the Danish King of York, but later accepted the protection of King Alfred of England. He visited Alfred's Court to pay homage (the first instance of Welsh agreement to pay homage to the English) and accepted English help against his aggressive brother Cadell. He was succeeded by his son IDWAL FOEL 916–942 (Idwal the Bald), who was eventually killed in rebellion against the English king Edmund I. His son IAGO 950–979 did not immediately inherit the territory, since he was run out of Gwynedd by the impetus of an invasion from the south led by Cadell's son, Rhodri's grandson, HYWEL DDA 909–950 (Hywel the Good). Hywel, lord of Deheubarth, had in 918 tactfully submitted to Edward the Elder of England and had been confirmed in his dominion. A sincere admirer of the English, he had copied the experience of his idol, King Alfred, and visited Rome. Later he led his chieftains in submission to King Æthelstan. But he was no habitual submitter. He expelled from Gwynedd and old Powys Iago and Ieuaf, the sons of Idwal Foel, and consolidated all Wales except Morgannwg and Gwent. After the death of Hywel Dda in 950,

Above left *Idwal Foel (Idwald the Bald), who was killed in revolt against Edmund I.*

Left *A delightful likeness of the sister of Idwal Foel.*

93

Iago and Ieuaf fought their way back into Gwynedd, defeating Hywel's son OWAIN 954–986. Then they fought among themselves, and Ieuaf's son HYWEL 979–985 (known as Hywel the Bad) emerged as lord of Gwynedd. He was succeeded by his brother CAD-WALLON 985–986, but Hywel Dda's grandson MAREDUDD AP OWAIN 986-989 drove up from the south and reunited Gwynedd with Deheubarth.

On the death of Maredudd in 999 Gwynedd reverted to Hywel the Bad's son CYNAN 999–1005, but Deheubarth lapsed into 20 years of anarchy during which no clear leader emerged.

Maredudd's son-in-law LLYWELYN AP SEISYLL 1018–1023 briefly rose from chaos and ruled Gwynedd as well as Deheubarth. But it was his son GRUFFYDD AP LLYWELYN 1039–1063 who, from his base in Gwynedd (for the territories were split again) fought a notable two-handed war against England and Deheubarth. He made extensive conquests along the Hereford border, ravaged Ceredigion, and finally secured Deheubarth. For a time Gruffydd was undisputed Ruler of All Wales, and in addition held exten-sive territory in Mercia, for which he nonchalantly swore loyalty to Edward the Confessor in return for recognition as under-king in Wales. His status was confirmed by his marriage to Ealdgyth, daughter of the Earl of Mercia. But in 1063 Earl Harold of Wessex, soon to be King Harold of England, attacked Wales by land and sea, fomented treachery within Wales, and was finally gratified by news of the death of Gruffydd at the hands of his own men. The troubled land immediately disintegrated into fragments once more.

At the same time, England was reeling under the Norman Conquest. William reckoned to keep the Welsh in check, if not in order, by creating three great feudal counties along the border, and passing the responsibility to their holders, the Earls of Chester, Shrews-bury and Hereford, who were entitled to keep any land or property which they could forage in Wales. The system worked well for some time, while the intimidated Welsh resorted to making war on each other. But in 1075 a remarkable blend of patriot and pirate arose in the person of GRUFFYDD AP CYNAN (ruled 1081–1137). He sprang from Gwynedd's royal line, the

Above *Gruffydd ap Llywelyn undisputed ruler of all Wales, married Ealdgyth of Mercia.*

Left *The ruins of White Castle near Abergavenny one of the forts of Southeast Wales.*

Opposite *Gruffydd ap Cynan, a powerful blend of patriot and pirate, attempted to take Gwynedd.*

dynasty of Idwal Foel, but he was born in Ireland, where his exiled father had married the daughter of the Scandinavian King Olaf of Dublin. In 1075 Gruffydd, aged 22, invaded Anglesey with an army of Irish and Norse mercenaries, and made an unsuccessful attempt to take over Gwynedd. He repeated the effort two years later, and again failed. But in 1081 he landed in the south-west and fought his way north to claim his title as lord of Gwynedd. Then the Normans captured him and imprisoned him in Chester.

After some years he escaped, gathered enough forces in Gwynedd for a successful plundering foray against nearby Norman property, and then retired to the Orkneys, where he fitted out a fleet of ships and made piratical lunges at Norman territory as far apart as Monmouth and Anglesey. Then he settled down in the north and systematically conquered Gwynedd by force of arms. He was considered so serious a menace to Norman stability that King William Rufus himself commanded two expeditions against him. Gruffydd merely withdrew his forces into the

security of the mountains and waited until the king went home again. He continued these tactics against King Henry I, though he did consent to meet the English monarch and pay homage for Gwynedd, reasoning that the act gave him a recognized right to hold his territories against the incursions of the Norman earls of the Marches.

Meanwhile in the south, a chief named RHYS AP TEWDWR 1081–1093 had been recognized by William the Conqueror as lord of Deheubarth on payment of £40 a year, a rent which is recorded in the *Domesday Book*. Rhys was killed in a skirmish with the Normans, and the security of Deheubarth grew rapidly uncertain. By 1135, when Gruffydd Ap Cynan was still ruling in Gwynedd, the south was virtually under total Norman rule.

On the death of King Henry I of England there was a general uprising in South Wales under GRUFFYDD AP RHYS 1135–1137 the son of Rhys Ap Tewdwr. Although he was eventually defeated and he died, the fight within Deheubarth was taken up by his three sons Cadell, Maredudd, and RHYS AP GRUFFYDD

1170–1197. In the north, the three sons of Gruffydd Ap Cynan – Cadwallon, OWAIN GWYNEDD 1137–1170 and Cadwaladr – were parallel nuisances within Gwynedd, and in turn their work was carried on by Owain's sons DAFYDD 1170–1194 and RHODRI AP OWAIN 1175–1195. In 1164–5 a north-south combination of Owain and his sons with Rhys Ap Gruffydd and other allies so completely countered a would-be punitive campaign by Henry II that the English king abandoned any attempt to conquer Wales in his lifetime.

When Owain Gwynedd died in 1170, strong leadership in Wales passed to the south, to Rhys Ap Gruffydd in Deheubarth. Henry II, who was in international ecclesiastical trouble over the murder of Becket, was glad to confirm the suzerainty of Rhys over all those territories which, a generation earlier, had been under Norman sway. The king actually appointed the Welshman as his Regent (Justiciar) in south Wales (including Ceredigion and Dyfed – Cardiganshire and Pembrokeshire), making all lesser chieftains vassals of Rhys, who was called The Lord Rhys from this time. This high status lasted for 17 years, until the death of Henry II in 1189. But the Anglo-Welsh understanding faded in the reign of Richard I, and with the death of Rhys another period of fragmentation seemed imminent.

Rescue came from Gwynedd, where LLYWELYN AP IORWERTH 1194– 1240, later known as Llywelyn the Great, was reasserting a central control of the territory after the fratricidal chaos that followed the death of his grandfather Owain Gwynedd. By 1201 he had established his own position as lord of West Gwynedd, and he had status enough for King John to propose a treaty with him. By 1204 he was controlling far more territory and, in return for homage to the English king, had taken John's illegitimate daughter Joan in marriage. He then took over Powys (which had slipped away from Gwynedd in the years of anarchy), and even Ceredigion. By 1210 John was finding his son-in-law far too powerful for a feudal vassal, and moved against him with military force. His total achievement, however, was that he united all Wales against himself. In 1215, the year of *Magna Carta* – which

restored, even to the Welsh, many privileges that had been taken from them during the years of war – Llywelyn moved against the royal castles in South Wales and took every garrison-point except Pembroke and Haverfordwest. Even Glamorgan was held by an English ally, the rebelling Earl of Essex. Llywelyn became in strict truth Ruler of All Wales.

There were later adjustments, disagreements, and the incessant private battles of ambitious English barons and jealous Welsh lords. But a peace was patched up, and was maintained for 15 years, under which Llywelyn was recognized as Ruler of Wales by the mystic title Prince of Aberffraw and Lord of Snowdon.

He died in 1240 and was briefly succeeded by his second son DAVID 1240–1246. David's successor was his nephew LLYWELYN AP GRUFFYDD 1246–1282, later to be known as Llywelyn the Last. The death of Llywelyn the Great had caused the partition of his hereditary territories in Gwynedd. Llywelyn the Last gradually built them together again. Then, by active military measures against King Henry III and combined military and diplomatic action against the Welsh chiefs, he reasserted his authority over the rest of Wales so successfully that, in 1258, with only one Welsh lord not paying homage to him, he declared himself Prince of Wales – with the utmost justification. By the Treaty of Pipton, July 19, 1265, this title was recognized by Simon de Montfort in the name of King Henry III (whom he was holding prisoner at this time of civil war). In addition, Simon agreed that his daughter Eleanor should be married to Llywelyn. (She was 13 years old at the time and Llywelyn was about 40. The marriage was celebrated, by proxy, ten years later in 1275, and consummated only in 1278. She died in childbirth in 1282). Almost immediately after the pact at Pipton, de Montfort was killed at the battle of Evesham. But Llywelyn fought on, and finally concluded the Treaty of Montgomery, September 25, 1267, whereby King Henry III, in return for homage, granted Llywelyn fresh lands, and confirmed in him and his heirs the title Prince of Wales.

Edward I succeeded to the English throne in 1272, and was content to

Left *Llywelyn ap Gruffydd who was recognized as Prince of Wales by Simon de Montfort.*

Opposite *One of the castles of the powerful Welsh princes of Gwynedd in Dolbarden, Caernarvonshire.*

Below *Llywelyn ap Iorwerth. Later known as Llywelyn the Great, he took King John's daughter in marriage.*

wait for internal Welsh disunity to topple Llywelyn. His policy was sound. Welsh lords – accustomed by their ancient laws to titular independence – would not maintain the loyalty of feudal vassalage to a Welsh Prince of Wales, and Llywelyn the Last could not frame a centralized administration which would hold the principality together. There were even Welsh conspiracies to assassinate him. And Llywelyn, losing his touch on statesmanship, allowed himself to be manoeuvred into a further military struggle against King Edward I. When Edward moved against him, half of Wales supported the English over-lord, and by 1277 the so-called Prince of Wales could control only Gwynedd. Edward then intensified a systematic destruction of Welsh liberties, and provoked a wide revolt in 1282.

By this time Llywelyn could not organize the Welsh even when they were fighting for their existence as a separate people. He himself was killed by an English scout during a skirmish in the south. His head was taken for display in Anglesey and later in London. Wales had lost more than a titular head. Her independence was gone for ever. Apart from the feudal estates of the Marches – which constitute a part of modern, but not old, Wales – she was annexed to the English crown. And it was in Pembrokeshire, a traditionally crown-dominated region, that Henry Tudor was born, in 1457, and landed 28 years later to march up the steps of the English throne. However, since he had been born and brought up in Wales, Henry was passionate in his constant assertion of his Welsh heritage.

Above *Llywellyn allowed his principality to disintegrate by internal friction.*

Left *The death of Llywelyn ap Gryffudd marked the end of Welsh independence.*

98

Henry VII
1485-1509

Born at Pembroke Castle on January 28, 1457.

Proclaimed himself as 'King of England and of France, Prince of Wales and Lord of Ireland' after the battle of Bosworth on August 22, 1485 at the age of 28.

The empty title of King of France was claimed as part of the style of all English monarchs before George IV, being formally renounced in 1802. But in this chronicle it is ignored henceforth as a serious statement.

Distant cousin of his predecessor Richard, who was a great-great-grandson of Edward III. Henry was a great-great-great-grandson of Edward III through his mother, a Beaufort, who was a great-granddaughter of John of Gaunt by his mistress Katherine Swynford, whose children were later legitimized.

The obstinate Beauforts, who tangled in the succession for a century, and finally founded a royal dynasty were, in seniority, 1. John, created Earl of Somerset, whose granddaughter Margaret married Edmund Tudor; 2. Henry, Cardinal Beaufort, Bishop of Winchester; 3. Thomas, Duke of Exeter; 4. Joan, whose second husband was Ralph Neville, Earl of Westmoreland and who was grandmother of Edward IV and of Warwick the King-Maker. The four original Beauforts were born to Katherine Swynford and John of Gaunt while John's second wife was still alive. On her death in 1394 John married Katherine, and in 1397 Richard II, as a favour to John of Gaunt and in order to neutralize John's son Derby (later King Henry IV) legitimized the children who had been born out of wedlock. Richard's Act of Parliament did not bar the Beauforts or their descendants from the throne. But Henry IV later wrote in, between the lines of the document, a clause excluding the Beauforts from the succession. This interlineation was, bluntly, a forgery of an Act of Parliament, and Henry VII's succession confounded it.

Married on January 18, 1486, when he

Above *Henry VII, first king of the House of Tudor.*

Below *Henry VII's chapel at Westminster Abbey is a fine example of Perpendicular Gothic architecture.*

was 28 and the bride was 20, after obtaining papal dispensation, his 'cousin' Elizabeth of York, eldest child of Edward IV and sister of Edward V. She died in 1503.

Children Arthur, Margaret, HENRY, Elizabeth, Mary, Edward, Catherine.

Died of gout aggravated into pneumonia, at Richmond, on April 5, 1509, aged 52, having reigned 23 years. Buried in Westminster Abbey.

Profile Medium height, reddish hair, worn long and combed back. Cleanshaven. At the time of his accession his grey eyes shone from an alert and mobile face, and his legs were easily coaxed into the dance or the hunt. Twenty years later, when gout had seriously affected him, his hair was sparse, though he was not bald. His gaze had grown shrewd and secretive, and his thin lips were sucked in over his few remaining teeth. Henry's interests were in hunting and lowbrow Court entertainments, but he did spend money freely on books. Intellectually, he was often crudely superstitious. He was not the miser which he is sometimes depicted: he lost £40 at cards in one day and he paid £30 to 'the young damsel that danceth' – about 60 times his usual payment to Court entertainers. Henry had a high standard of living, and it was only his genius for amassing money that brought his affluence.

꧁ꩰꧏꩰꧏꩰꧏꩰꧏꩰꧏꩰꧏꩰ꧂

Henry was the unorthodox offspring of the clandestine (but valid) marriage between Henry V's widow, Catherine of Valois, and a dashing Welshman who had been a gentleman usher at her Court, Sir Owen Tudor. The elder son of this marriage, Henry's father Edmund Tudor, was thus half-brother to King Henry VI and was created Earl of Richmond by him, Edmund married the king's cousin, Lady Margaret Beaufort, heiress of John Duke of Somerset, grandson to John of Gaunt, and he died while Margaret was pregnant with their only child. Henry was born in Wales, with Welsh ancestry, spent all his youth in Wales (and none in England), and devoted a fervour, which was as near to the romantic as his character would permit, to declaring himself a Welshman. But after the blood-bath of Lancastrian heirs and leaders which followed the battle of Tewkesbury, Henry, as the senior survivor, was sent

abroad to France. He was 14 years old, and he lived in a penurious and sometimes hazardous exile – which coloured his later life more remarkably even than the long exile of Charles II before the Restoration. It was a calculating and suspicious man of 28 who returned to win the throne in 1485.

Henry IV, in similar circumstances, announced that he held the crown by the decision of Parliament. Henry VII explicitly denied this, and told Parliament that he held the crown 'by just heredity and the judgement of God' – the old Norman argument that God's wisdom had ordained his victory at Bosworth. The papal bull granting dispensation for his marriage to Elizabeth of York did, however, mention a legal sanction, declaring that he held the throne by the rights of conquest, inheritance, election (acclamation), and Act of Parliament. But Henry ignored Parliament as much as he conveniently could, and summoned it only for total

Above *Elizabeth, wife of Henry VII.*

Opposite *An indenture, signed by Henry VII and his clergy, licensing functions at Westminster Abbey.*

sittings of ten months during his 23-years reign. He was mainly able to achieve this by keeping out of the heavy expenses of war, and perfecting his own efficient and ruthless methods of collecting revenue, which put the national accounts into a £1½million surplus by the time he died.

As an alternative to war, Henry pursued a policy of dynastic marriages. His children were eventually used to cement alliances with Spain, Scotland and France. But it was his reckless manipulation of the young Catherine of Aragon – whom he once contemplated marrying himself – which provided the powder for the great ecclesiastical explosion of the following reign.

Henry VIII
1509-1547

Known (only in retrospect) as Bluff King Hal

Born at Greenwich on June 28, 1491.

Succeeded as King of England and Lord of Ireland on April 5, 1509 at the age of 17. Henry styled himself King of Ireland from 1544.

Second son (of three) but only surviving son of his predecessor Henry.

Married 1. on 11 June 1509, when he was 18 and the bride was 24, the widow of his elder brother Arthur, Catherine of Aragon, daughter of King Ferdinand V of Aragon and II of Sicily. He finally separated from her in 1531, and the marriage was annulled by English law in May 1533. She died in January 1536; 2. secretly in January 1533, when he was 41 and she was 26, and she was pregnant with Elizabeth, Anne Boleyn, daughter of the Earl of Wiltshire and niece of the Duke of Norfolk. She was beheaded on 19 May 1536; 3. in May 1536, when he was 44 and she was 27, Jane Seymour, daughter of Sir John Seymour. She died after childbirth in October 1537; 4. in January 1540, when he was 48 and she was 25, Anne of Cleves, daughter of the Duke of Cleves (on the Rhine). The marriage was annulled in July 1540. She died at Chelsea in 1557; 5. secretly in November 1540, when he was 49 and she was 17, Catherine Howard, niece of the Duke of Norfolk. She was beheaded on 13 February 1542; 6. in 1543 when he was 51 and she was 31, Catherine Parr, widow of Lord Latimer. She survived him, and in the year of Henry's death married Jane Seymour's brother Thomas Seymour, Lord Admiral of England, who had previously proposed to Princess Elizabeth, later Elizabeth I. She died after childbirth in September 1548. Seymour again proposed to Elizabeth, and was executed in January 1549.

Children (discounting those still-born or dying in extreme infancy): of Catherine of Aragon: MARY of Anne Boleyn: ELIZABETH of Jane Seymour: EDWARD.

Mistresses Elizabeth Blount, Mary Boleyn.

Bastard Henry Fitzroy, Duke of Richmond, by Elizabeth Blount.

Died at Westminster of kidney disease, gout and a circulatory disorder, exacerbated by a tortuously painful leg ulcer, on January 28, 1547, at the age of 55, having reigned 37 years. Buried at Windsor.

Profile 6ft tall, fair skin, auburn hair, blue eyes. His hair was gradually

Opposite *Henry VIII surrounded by five of his wives. Reading clockwise, they are Jane Seymour, Anne of Cleves, Catherine of Aragon, Catherine Parr, and Catherine Howard. A complex man, Henry allowed his desire for a male heir to become an overriding obsession.*

Below *Hampton Court, built by Cardinal Wolsey.*

102

KATHARINE PARRE

Opposite *Anne Boleyn was a victim of Henry's fanatical desire for a male heir. She bore him a girl.*

Above *The initials of King Henry VIII and Anne Boleyn, which can be seen at King's College Chapel.*

Right *Henry and Cardinal Wolsey who also fell victim to the king's ambitions and temperament.*

worn shorter as he grew older. In his late twenties he grew the beard for which he is now memorable, and English Court fashion followed this trend. He was very sturdy, and excelled at all sports. He was a practical musician and a tireless dancer. In later life he became bald and grotesquely fat. He was an accomplished linguist and of considerable intellectual stature, especially in theology. In character he was self-indulgent, and ruthless against anyone posing a challenge to his authority. 'Heads will fly' was his own phrase.

ⱥⱥⱥⱥⱥⱥⱥⱥⱥⱥⱥⱥⱥⱥⱥ

Henry, as the second son of his father, was not at first groomed for the throne but for the chair of the Archbishop of Canterbury, and his proficiency at learning seemed to justify that decision. When he was ten, his elder brother Arthur (zealously given by his Welsh father the name of the old British King) was married to Catherine of Aragon. But Arthur died in the following year, and the widowed Catherine, aged 18, was betrothed to the 12-year-old Henry, now Prince of Wales. The principal reason for this fateful match, which was dubious according to the Church's rules on affinity, seems to have been that

Henry VII did not want to renounce Catherine's dowry. Henry VIII celebrated the marriage six years later, after his accession.

His first ambition as sovereign was to be the Arbiter of Europe, negotiating – and intriguing – between the international political personalities of the time: his father-in-law Ferdinand of Aragon, his relation by marriage the Emperor Maximilian, Pope Julius II and King Louis XII of France. This culminated in a profitable short war in France which was characteristically patched up by marrying Henry's sister Mary to the French King. This was Henry VIII's barren legacy from the dynastic ambitions of his father (for Louis died almost immediately). During Henry's absence fighting in France the Earl of Surrey defeated and killed Henry's brother-in-law King James IV of Scotland at the battle of Flodden in 1513, after which there was peace with Scotland for nearly 30 years.

Henry then apparently abandoned Europe, although without overconcentrating on the affairs of England. The truth was that he left home and foreign policy almost exclusively to his Chancellor, Thomas Wolsey, an arrogant and avaricious man who wanted to net the posts of Emperor for Henry and Pope for himself. (Yet he had held the Archbishopric of York for 15 years before he visited the Minster, during his final disgrace).

Queen Catherine had borne a series of sickly or still-born children, and only a girl survived, whom Henry could not accept as his heir. Wolsey encouraged Henry to write the theological work against the church-reforming doctrines of Luther which gained him the papal accolade of the title *Defender of the Faith*, still retained by his successors today – and about as inapposite as the claim to be King of France. During the research and meditation necessary for this serious publication, Henry developed genuine doubts about the validity of his marriage to Catherine. These coincided with a genuine lust for other women and a superstitious, but not ridiculous, belief that his wife's inability to bear healthy males was a sign of God's displeasure at the union. Henry instructed Cardinal Wolsey to press the Pope to annul the dispensation of a previous Pope permitting Henry's marriage to his deceased brother's widow. What Julius II had permitted Clement VII could cancel – but Pope Clement had just cautiously emerged from being the literal, military, prisoner of the Emperor Charles V, who was the nephew of Catherine of Aragon and who understandably instructed Clement VII in papal infallibility. After two years' scheming, Wolsey failed to secure the annulment of Henry's marriage, and he was ruined and died.

Sir Thomas More succeeded him as Chancellor, Thomas Cromwell as chief minister. Cromwell pushed through the attack on papal domination which led to the bishops' recognition of Henry as Supreme Head of the Church of England and, later, to the bishops' annulment of the marriage of Henry and Catherine. Henry had already secretly married Anne Boleyn, and in September 1533 she bore a child. The baby was female, the next miscarried, and the next was still-born. Henry, urgently desiring a male heir, had Anne executed for

alleged incest and adultery (having previously had the marriage annulled), and he married Jane Seymour, who bore him a son and died in childbirth.

Meanwhile Henry's almost maniacal tyranny had removed by execution state officers like Sir Thomas More who could not accept the *spiritual* (rather than temporal) privileges he claimed in opposition to the Pope, together with aristocrats who might possibly head a dynastic revolt against his tenure of the throne. The next to go to the block was Cromwell, after he had completed the enormous increase in the king's wealth which resulted from the dissolution of the monasteries. Cromwell blundered. by binding Henry almost irrevocably to take the unseen, unseductive (but politically acceptable, as a Lutheran Catholic) Anne of Cleves as his fourth wife. Henry got Thomas Cranmer, Archbishop of Canterbury, to record his third annulment of a royal marriage, and Cranmer next connived at the execution for immorality of Henry's fifth wife, the teenaged Catherine Howard. The last wife, Catherine Parr, a tactful manager except for her propensity to provoke Henry with arguments on theology, narrowly escaped arrest by his 'Thought Police', and outlived him.

Catherine Parr, like many in England in this time of fundamental religious rethinking, was more radically Protestant than the king. Apart from the issue of his supremacy, Henry did not diverge

far from basic Catholic doctrine. But he had it expressed in English, through the use of the translated Bible and Cranmer's deathless contribution to the Litany and the Book of Common Prayer (the latter not issued until 1549). Radical Protest-

ants incited diehard reaction among old Catholics, and when Henry died the stage was set for extremism. Also, he was so extravagant a monarch that when he died the treasury was virtually empty and the coinage debased.

Above *Edward VI painted by a follower of Hans Holbein, dated about 1550 when the boy was 13 years old.*

Right *A fascinating glimpse of the exercise book of Edward VI showing his Latin script.*

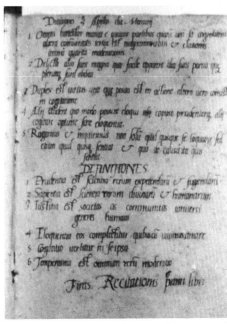

Opposite above *Henry VIII meets Francis I of France. Both were absolutist monarchs.*

Opposite below *The official Coat of Arms of Henry VIII.*

Edward VI
1547-1553

Born at Hampton Court on October 12, 1537, his mother, Jane Seymour, dying 12 days later.

Succeeded as King of England and Ireland on January 28, 1547 at the age of nine.

Only surviving son and only legitimate son – only legitimate child, according to retrospective Acts of Parliament pushed through by Henry – of his predecessor Henry. (Henry's son by Elizabeth Blount, Henry Fitzroy, Duke of Richmond, who died in 1536 aged about 20, had had a good chance of succeeding to the throne).

Betrothed at the age of six to Mary Queen of Scots, then only a few months old. But this engagement was repudiated by the Scots who married Mary to the Dauphin of France. Edward did not marry.

Died of tuberculosis at Greenwich on July 6, 1553, aged 15, having reigned six years. Buried in King Henry VII's Chapel in Westminster Abbey.

Profile Small stature, pale face, with red hair cut short. A devoted scholar and a keen Protestant. He had an autocratic nature which accepted the execution of ambitious Protestant statesmen.

🙟🙟🙟🙟🙟🙟🙟🙟🙟🙟🙟

As a devout, even puritan, Protestant, Edward sanctioned the promotion of his mother's brothers, the Seymours, to the highest offices of state, but acquiesced in their subsequent liquidation. Power was then taken by John Dudley, Duke of Northumberland, who married his son Guildford to Edward's cousin Jane Grey, and persuaded Edward to nominate Jane as his heir. Mary, daughter of Henry VIII and Catherine of Aragon, and Elizabeth, daughter of Henry and Anne Boleyn, had been declared illegitimate by Act of Parliament of 1536. The nomination of Lady Jane Grey, who was Henry VII's great-granddaughter was designed to secure the succession of a Protestant. It also served to further the ambitions of Northumberland, for in arranging the marriage of his son to Lady Jane, he was manouvering for dynastic power.

Jane
1553

Known as the Nine Days Queen

Born at Bradgate, Leicestershire in 1537.
Proclaimed secretly as Queen of England and Ireland on July 6, 1553. Proclaimed publicly in London on July 10, 1553 at the age of 16. Sent to the Tower of London on July 19, 1553 having reigned nine days.
First cousin of her predecessor Edward, being granddaughter of Henry VIII's sister Mary, who was briefly Queen of France and then Countess of Suffolk. Mary's daughter Frances married Henry Grey who became Duke of Suffolk. Jane was their eldest daughter.
Married in 1553, before her accession, at the age of 16, Lord Guildford Dudley, aged about 19, youngest son of the Duke of Northumberland.
Died Executed by beheading at the Tower of London on February 12, 1554 at the age of 16.
Profile Slim figure, brown hair worn tight to the head and deliberately not curled. Conscientiously modest in dress and appearance, though a state portrait gives her plucked, arched eyebrows.

༝༚༝༚༝༚༝༚༝༚༝༚༝༚

Shortly before the death of Edward VI, the Duke of Northumberland, controlling the government, persuaded the king to sign a will which passed over six possible claimants to the throne and assigned the succession to Northumberland's daughter-in-law, Jane. On the death of Edward Northumberland tried to kidnap the heir with the strongest claim, Mary, eldest child of Henry VIII. Mary evaded him and the country rose against him. He was taken prisoner at Cambridge on the day of the proclamation of Mary as queen. Within five weeks Northumberland had been executed, and Jane and her husband were prisoners in the Tower. Five months later, after a revolt occasioned by Mary's announcement that she would marry Philip of Spain, Jane was executed, along with her husband and father and some 60 others. Rather than demonstrating any personal ambition of her own, Jane was the unfortunate victim of the dynastic power game.

Left *Sir Thomas Wyatt, poet and courtier and lover of Anne Boleyn, survived Henry VIII's displeasure. His son, also Sir Thomas, narrowly failed to overthrow Mary I in 1554 and was executed for high treason.*

Below *Lady Jane Grey, the 'Nine Days Queen' was nominated by the young King Edward as his heir.*

Opposite above *Mary I enters London in triumph in 1553 with her sister Elizabeth.*

Mary
1553-1558

Known as Bloody Mary

Born at Greenwich on February 18, 1516.
Succeeded as Queen of England and Ireland on July 19, 1553 at the age of 37. On her marriage to Philip she was grandiosely styled Queen of England, France, Naples, Jerusalem and Ireland.
Half-sister of King Edward VI and daughter of Henry VIII.
Married in Winchester Cathedral in July 1554, when she was 38 and he was 27, Philip of Spain, son of the Emperor Charles V, who nominated him King of Naples for his wedding and, abdicating two years later, made him King of Spain and the wide Spanish possessions. By the agency of death, not divorce, Philip had four wives: Catherine of Portugal, Mary of England, Elizabeth of France and Anne of Austria.
Children None.
Died at St James's Palace, of pneumonia after a long history of illness including amenorrhoea and heart disease presenting as dropsy, on November 17, 1558, aged 42, having reigned five years. Buried in King Henry VII's Chapel, Westminster Abbey.
Profile Short stature, undeveloped figure, red hair, pale face, dark eyes which became short-sighted and red-rimmed. A thin mouth pursed over too few teeth. In delicate health from her teens, she was always elaborately dressed, her costume displaying her passion for jewels. A very good linguist, a fair musician, intelligent in argument, dignified and courageous, but because she was barren, thwarted and bitter. A devout Catholic whose religious and political life was oppressed by the scandalous treatment of her mother, Catherine of Aragon.

🙦🙤🙦🙤🙦🙤🙦🙤🙦🙤🙦🙤

Mary's adolescence was inevitably tainted by Henry's humiliating repudiation of her mother and herself, and by persecution from Anne Boleyn, who hounded her as a bastard, little knowing that her own daughter Elizabeth was to receive the same treatment. In her defense, Mary clung more fiercely to the old Catholic faith and to the sup-

Below *Philip and Mary's Coat of Arms. Mary's marriage to the Spanish king was a crucial Catholic alliance.*

Below *Philip advised against Mary's vicious heresy-hunt in England on political grounds.*

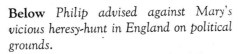

remacy of the Pope, though she never lost an intense regard for the majesty radiated by the person of her father. After the death of Catherine, Mary made, under Catholic advice, a serious compromise. She acknowledged her mother's divorce and recognized Henry's supplanting of the Pope, making her oath of loyalty to her father as Supreme Head of the English Church. Suppressed guilt at this surrender may have hardened her reaction when she became queen. (But at no time did she renounce her own position as Head of the Church).

During the reign of her brother Edward, who was himself a somewhat precocious partisan Protestant, harassment of Mary as a Catholic increased. Yet when she first came to the throne, her policies were mild enough, though she did not disguise her intention to restore Catholicism within England by re-introducing the Mass, reinstating all deprived bishops, and expelling those of the clergy who had married. But an early revolt against her proposed 'Spanish marriage' was put down with more aristocratic and other heads flying than her father or her brother had ever ordered. And the marriage itself was followed by an intensification of heresy-hunting and the first executions of clerics by burning at the stake – atrocities which Philip himself strongly counselled against in England, on political rather than humanitarian grounds, for in the Netherlands he was burning five for every one Mary burnt in England.

After 14 months of marriage, Philip left England. He returned only once, to bully Mary into declaring war on France – and thus into losing Calais after an English tenure of 211 years. Mary never conceived a child, though she sometimes deluded herself that she was pregnant. Her personal bitterness increased. The burnings of the Protestants became more frequent. After Archbishop Cranmer – who, in spite of his moral timidity towards Henry VIII, had once saved Mary from the execution block by pleading with her father – and after the bishops and clergy, there came a succession of 200 simple men, and over 60 women, who had for the most part merely read the Bible and made up their own minds about their faith. Their deaths, above all else, forged the steel of the Church of England.

Below *An Elizabethan-style monument for Princess Mary, daughter of James I.*

Opposite *Walter Raleigh and his son.*

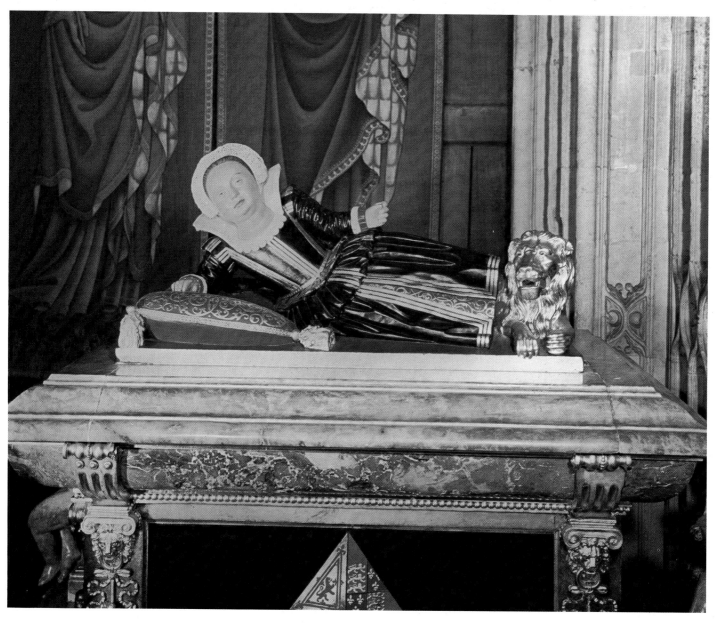

Elizabeth I
1558-1603

Known as the Virgin Queen

Born at Greenwich on September 7, 1533.
Succeeded as Queen of England and Ireland on November 17, 1558 at the age of 25.
Half-sister of her predecessor Mary, and daughter of Henry VIII and Anne Boleyn.
Marriage None.
Died at Richmond of old age, specifically of pneumonia following a chill, on March 24, 1603, aged 69, having reigned 44 years. Buried in King Henry VII's Chapel in Westminster Abbey.
Profile Above medium height, fair complexion, hazel eyes which darkened over the years, yellow-red hair later covered by a vivid auburn wig. Thin lips, bad teeth which became black in age. As queen, she was always ornately dressed with a profusion of jewels. Foreign ambassadors complained that even in her sixties, 'following the fashion of unmarried ladies in England', she kept her wrinkled bosom uncovered, but her official portraits do not show this. She was learned in six languages but had little taste for art or literature. Though she could assume majesty at any time, her language and her manners were coarse, and at Court she could instil as much fear as her father had done. She was, by force of circumstance, a dissembling politician, constantly manipulating people, but as a schemer she was disabled by her vacillation: she hated to make a firm decision, particularly at times of crisis. She was coquettish, craved flattery, and with the inherent highly-charged sexual drive of the Tudors she undoubtedly lost her heart on occasions. But there is no reliable ground for disbelieving her strong assertion that she never surrendered her body.

꜀꜀꜀꜀꜀꜀꜀꜀꜀꜀꜀꜀

Elizabeth had a clouded birth and a wretched childhood. Her mother was beheaded before she was three. She was immediately designated a bastard, but not expelled from the royal circle, and she later became the affectionate protegée of her two surviving stepmothers, Anne

Opposite *Elizabeth I of England, resplendent in her jewels, captured the imagination of her subjects.*

Above *Thomas Cromwell, chief minister to Henry VIII, led the attack on papal authority over the English throne.*

of Cleves and Catherine Parr. She was on friendly terms with her half-sister Mary, 14 years her senior, and with her young half-brother Edward, who, however, demanded extravagant obeisance once he was king. On the advice of William Cecil, Secretary of State under Edward, she kept out of inflammatory politics and, at the beginning of Mary's reign, survived the move to have her executed with Jane after Sir Thomas Wyatt's revolt in favour of her accession. She swore to Mary that she was 'a true Roman Catholic', but on her (undisputed) acces-

sion to the throne, though she appointed both Catholics and Protestants indifferently to her Council, some Catholic bishops found themselves in the Tower with the introduction of a revised English-language Book of Common Prayer. This modified the more extreme protestantism of Edward's book, but recognized Elizabeth as Head of the Church.

Elizabeth, though not deeply religious, would have been classed in later days as an Anglo-Catholic. The politics of the time, affecting both the international scene and the question of the succession to the English throne, drove the Roman Catholic cause into the area of treason. The claimants to the throne were Catholics: Philip II of Spain as the husband of Queen Mary Tudor, and Mary Queen of Scots, who was in any case the Heir Presumptive and, as great-grand-daughter of Henry VII, had a strong claim to immediate possession if she asserted Elizabeth's illegitimacy – which she promptly did. When Mary was expelled from Scotland and took refuge in England, English Catholics intrigued for her immediate succession and the international Catholic powers, Rome, France and Spain, financed and elaborated these intrigues. The political situation was inflamed by the genuine religious reformation and revival in the Catholic Church which resulted in the Jesuit missions to England and Ireland.

Reenthused English Catholics could become political conspirators, and some did, particularly after the bull of Pope Pius V which condoned the murder of Elizabeth. The queen increasingly moved against them for treason, though it is fair to say that the politico-religious executions in her reign of 44 years were no more in number than the burnings of the heretics during five years under Mary. In Ireland, where both the mood of the people and the risk of foreign intervention were more severe, Elizabeth's repression was savage, and permanently affected Anglo-Irish relations.

In her personal character, Elizabeth showed less than admirable traits in her handling of the execution of Mary Queen of Scots (popular though it was in the country) and of the challenge of the Spanish Armada, a long-standing threat which she would not acknowledge, so that she ran down her navy to the point where it could not exploit the victory gained by its seamanship. Though Elizabeth's foreign policy depended on maintaining peace, she was involved in expeditionary wars in France and

Top *Shakespeare was the major literary figure of the Elizabethan age, and fully expressed its complexity.*

Above *Lord Burleigh was the most influential advisor to Elizabeth as her Secretary of State.*

Opposite right *Archbishop Thomas Cranmer was one of Henry VIII's puppet clerics and a powerful Elizabethan.*

the Netherlands, and exacted a high dividend from the perquisites of licensed privateering against the Spanish treasure-ships. Keeping the peace demanded much playing for time – and the bait she used to spin out time was herself. Unlike Henry VII, she had no daughters to deal out in successive dynastic marriages: she had only herself, and she could be caught only once. So she offered herself and withdrew, flirted and stamped her foot, at different times with four kings of Europe. She even offered to Mary Queen of Scots the only man she would willingly have married: Robert Dudley, Earl of Leicester, ironically the brother of that Guildford Dudley who had married Jane Grey to exalt his father – but North-umberland had been beheaded long before he could manipulate Elizabeth's passion for Robert.

At home, Elizabeth also had to play for time, to heal sectarian wounds and to give her able ministers a space to get the country's economy on a prosperous course. She was given time – 44 years. In a sense she reigned too long. For, after

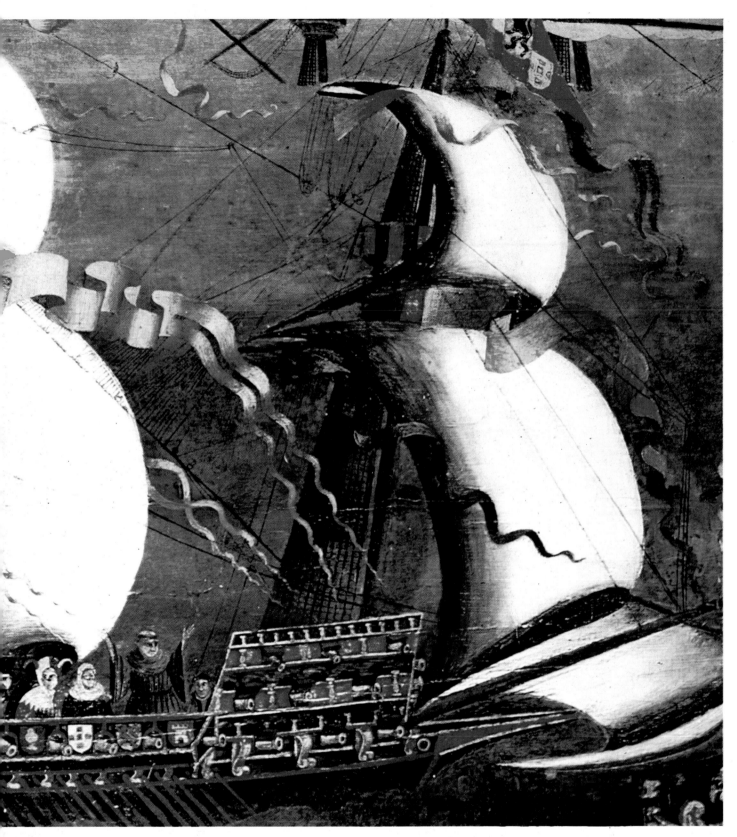

years spent stabilizing the country, and further years shared with the nation in a glorious self-confidence and zest, towards the end of her reign she understandably could not break away from a habitual despotism which was not always benevolent. She debased a proud people, under-used an intellectual middle class, and humiliated a Parliament which had grown in its potential to govern through the maturity that had perhaps only come to it so swiftly because of the stability she had previously given it. This simmering cauldron of problems she left to her successor to ladle. As an old woman with a momentous family story of sorrow and joy and achievement that was intimately shared in the family memory of all her subjects, much indulgence could be given her. A chord of truth found resonance in many hearts when she told her last Parliament: 'This I count the glory of my reign – that I have reigned with your loves.'

Above *A galleas,* Spanish fighting ship.

The Monarchs of Scotland

The natural and accepted heir to Queen Elizabeth was King James VI of Scotland, who came to Westminster as James I of England, to be crowned, as he called it, King of Great Britain, (though the archaic style was also used: 'King of England, Scotland, France and Ireland'). With this peaceful union of the crowns of England and Scotland it is fitting to record the previous Monarchs of Scotland.

Scotland – or *Scotia* – was the name originally given to Ireland. The Scots, who were Christians speaking Gaelic, came from Ireland and settled in modern Argyll and the islands to the west. To the east and north of them lived the Picts, so called by the Romans because they were *picti*, painted, when they went to war. South of the river Forth lived the Angles, on the east above Hadrian's Wall, and the Britons (who spoke Welsh) in the valley of the Clyde, with Dunbarton as their capital, in the kingdom called Strathclyde. By degrees the Scots and the Britons converted the neighbouring peoples to Christianity. But in the eighth century the native Celtic Church yielded its influence to the Roman Church.

In 843 KENNETH MACALPIN 843–860, who was King of the Scots, became also King of the Picts, and the united kingdom was called Alban. His daughter married the King of Strathclyde, and their son reigned briefly. But, although a continuous succession of kings can be traced from 843, the territory of Alban did not always include Strathclyde, and never decisively controlled Lothian (where the Angles lived between the Forth and the Tweed) for 130 years.

In 1018 MALCOLM II 1005–1034 conquered the Angles of Lothian at the battle of Carham, on the Tweed, and in the same year became legitimate heir to the kingdom of Strathclyde, now called Cumbria. The four Scottish kingdoms were united under Malcolm's grandson and successor, DUNCAN I 1034–1040. Duncan, who, a youth, not a dotard as Shakespeare tells the story, was challenged by MACBETH 1040–1057. Macbeth was the victor and reigned for 17 years before Duncan's son MALCOLM III 1057–1093 (known as

Opposite above The four Scottish kingdoms were united under Duncan I.

Opposite left Macbeth defeated Duncan and took the throne.

Opposite right King Alexander.

Big Head) raised a mixed force of Scots and English and killed him in battle. Malcolm had spent 15 years in exile at the Court of Edward the Confessor. He was English-speaking, Anglophile, and favoured English-speaking Lothian rather than his hereditary northern territories. This was an over-mixed

blessing for the people of Lothian, who had to endure the backlash of five invasions of Northumbria by Malcolm. These ended with Malcolm's recognition of William the Conqueror as his liege lord, (his great-grandfather Malcolm II had previously paid homage to Canute in 1031). They also led to the subsequent seizure of Cumberland from the Strathclyde territory in 1092 by William Rufus, who capped his father's creation of Newcastle by establishing Carlisle as a border fortress. Malcolm married Margaret, the sister of Edgar ÆTHELING, the Saxon heir of Edward the Confessor. She exerted a considerable, and often resented, English influence on the Scottish Church and Court. She was officially canonized as a saint in 1250.

Malcolm died during his last campaign against Northumbria, at the battle of Alnwick, November 13, 1093, aged about 62, and he was buried at Tynemouth and afterwards at Dunfermline. A period of confusion followed, with the kingdom being briefly ruled by Donald Bane, Duncan II and Edmund, the brother and sons of Malcolm. William Rufus solved this weakness by giving an army to a younger son, EDGAR 1097–1107, who took the kingdom and bequeathed it to his younger brother ALEXANDER I 1107–1124. He in turn passed it to a further brother, DAVID I 1124–1153, who pulled the troubled kingdom together.

David had ruled Cumbria and South Lothian since 1107, when Edgar had died after dividing the kingdom between his two younger brothers. He had spent his youth as a refugee at the Court of King Henry I of England, who had married his sister Eadgyth (or Matilda, or Maud) and fathered David's niece the Empress Matilda (Maud). David took advantage of the civil war between Matilda and Stephen to take over Northumbria coast-to-coast, He ignored the forts of Newcastle and Bamburgh, and in the 14 years of peace which followed he stamped the feudal system on to the body of Southern Scotland.

David died at Carlisle on May 24, 1153 aged about 73, having reigned 29 years, and was buried at Dunfermline. He was succeeded by his grandson MALCOLM IV 1153–1165, known as the Maiden on account of his appearance and the fact that he died unmarried (though he did

Above *The Kelso Charter between David I and Malcolm IV.*

Below *David I built this beautiful abbey on the River Jed.*

have an illegitimate son). He succeeded at the age of 11, and four years later ceded the counties of Northumbria, Cumberland and Westmoreland to King Henry II of England in exchange for the earldom of Huntingdon. His brother WILLIAM I 1165–1214 (known as William the Lion) was captured during an attempt to regain the territory, and was released by Henry II only on condition that he acknowledged Henry as Lord of Scotland and ruled as a vassal king. But he bought back his independence by a payment of 10,000 marks to the needy Richard Coeur de Lion.

William died at Stirling on December 4, 1214 aged 71, having reigned 48 years, and was buried at Arbroath. He was succeeded by his son ALEXANDER II 1214–1249, who married Joan, the daughter of King John of England. He died at the age of 50 on the island of Kerrera on an expedition to recapture the Hebrides from Norwegian rule, and was buried at Melrose. His son ALEXANDER III 1249–1286 acquired the Western Isles and the Isle of Man by treaty with Norway in 1266. Alexander married Margaret, sister of King Edward I of England, and their daughter Margaret married the King of Norway in 1281. Their daughter, also Margaret, was recognized as heir to the Scottish throne, and titularly succeeded when Alexander was killed by a fall from his horse near Kinghorn on March 19, 1286, aged 44 and having reigned 36 years.

Margaret, 'the Maid of Norway', was three years old. When she was six she was betrothed to Edward of Caernarvon, son of King Edward I of England. Next year she sailed from Norway, but died in Orkney on September 26, 1290, aged eight, after a reign of four years. She was buried in Bergen.

Thirteen claimants, then known as the Competitors, contested the throne. King Edward I of England was asked to arbitrate. He agreed to do so if his position as Overlord were restated, and as a pledge he took the castles of Scotland. Edward appointed a commission of experts which took some two years to report. The strongest candidates were descended from daughters of David, Earl of Huntingdon, 70 years dead and the brother of King William the Lion. Edward followed his commission's recommendation, and appointed

Above *William I, known as William the Lion.*

Below *Alexander III.*

Below *Scone Castle where Scottish kings were normally crowned.*

Bottom left *Carlisle Castle, where King David I resided in 1138.*

Bottom right *John Balliol was appointed king by Edward I.*

JOHN BALLIOL 1292–1296, grandson of the eldest daughter, in preference to Robert Bruce, son of the second daughter.

John Balliol therefore did homage to King Edward and was crowned at Scone. He showed that he had little authority against his own nobles and little dignity vis-a-vis the English king. But he defied Edward to the point of war, and in 1295 made the first of many treaties between Scotland and France, and against England, which were to fill the archives of the next three centuries. Edward moved against him and, with the help of Scottish nobles including Robert Bruce, Earl of Carrick, son of the Competitor, won the battle of Dunbar and forced John Balliol to abdicate in humiliating circumstances. Edward removed the Stone of Destiny from Scone and ran Scotland as a colony. He had the acquiescence of land-owning nobles, but met sporadic resistance from Sir William Wallace, who used terroristic methods until his betrayal and execution in 1305.

Robert I
1306-1329

Known as Robert the Bruce

Born at Writtle, near Chelmsford, Essex on July 11, 1274.

Assumed the Crown of Scotland at Scone on March 27, 1306 at the age of 31.

Grandson of Robert de Bruce, Lord of Annandale, who was grandson of Isabella, niece of King William I (the Lion). Earl of Carrick by inheritance through his mother.

(The Earldom of Carrick has been zealously restricted to the British Royal.

Family since the sentiment paid to the Scottish connection was recognized, and is at present held by the Prince of Wales).

Married 1. in 1295, Isabella, daughter of the Earl of Mar. She died at a date unknown; 2. in 1302, Elizabeth, daughter of the Earl of Ulster. She died in 1327.

Children of Isabella: Marjorie (founder of the Stewart line).
of Elizabeth: Matilda, DAVID, Margaret, John.

Bastards among others, Robert, Nigel, Margaret, Elizabeth, Christian.

Died at Cardross, Dumbartonshire, on June 7, 1329, aged 54, having reigned 23 years. Buried at Dunfermline. His heart was taken towards the Holy Land by Sir James Douglas, who was killed fighting the Moors in Spain, and the heart was brought back and buried at Melrose.

ﾃﾞﾞﾞﾞﾞﾞﾞﾞﾞﾞﾞﾞﾞﾞ

During the kingless Interregnum, 1296–1306, three Guardians of the Kingdom had been appointed by a Council of Magnates. Two of these, Robert Bruce and Sir John Comyn, quarrelled at the council. Six years later, on February 10, 1306, Bruce stabbed Comyn in a convent church at Dumfries, and was eventually excommunicated by the Pope for murder and sacrilege. Bruce, who had been seeking the crown alongside Comyn, claimed the throne and was crowned at Scone amid a very sparse assembly of nobles. Bruce had to flee the country when Edward pursued him, and the English king imprisoned his wife and sisters, and executed three of his brothers. After seven years of developing resistance, Bruce expelled the English from Scotland by his victory over Edward II at Bannockburn, near Stirling, on June 24, 1314. Robert then supported his brother Edward's invasion of Ireland, where Edward became king from 1316 to 1318 until he was killed by the English. A succession of bloody expeditions against northern England ended with the recognition by Edward III of the independence of Scotland in the treaty of Northampton, May 4, 1328, sealed by the marriage of Robert's heir David to Joanna, sister of the English King. The stipulation that the Stone of Destiny should be returned to Scone was defied by the Abbot of Westminster, and none of Robert's successors sat on it until James VI and I.

Above *Melrose abbey where the heart of Robert Bruce is supposed to be buried.*

Opposite above *Robert Stuart. The Scots meaning of Stuart is 'steward'.*

Opposite below *David II of Scotland in battle at Newcastle.*

Left *Robert Bruce, hero of Scotland at Bannockburn.*

Below *A fine view of the castle at Edinburgh which houses the Scottish royal jewels.*

David II
1329-1371

Born in Dunfermline on March 5, 1324.
Succeeded as King of Scots on June 7, 1329 at the age of five.
Son of his predecessor Robert by his second wife Elizabeth.
Married 1. on July 17, 1328, when he was four years old and she was about seven, Joanna, daughter of King Edward II of England. At Scone, on November 24, 1331 at the ages of seven and ten, both were crowned after being anointed (for the first time at Scottish coronations) with holy oil sent by the Pope, at the price of 12,000 gold florins. Joanna died in London in 1362; 2. in December 1363, Margaret Drummond, widow of Sir John Logie. He divorced her in March 1370. She successfully appealed to the Pope against the divorce, and died in Avignon in 1375.
Children None.
Died in Edinburgh Castle on February 22, 1371, aged 46 and having reigned 41 years. Buried at Holyrood.

❧❧❧❧❧❧❧❧❧❧❧

Three years after the accession of the boy King David, Edward Balliol, son of John Balliol, landed in Fife with English-orientated barons of Scotland. He beat the Scots army at Dupplin Moor and was crowned king at Scone on September 24, 1332. Before the year was out he was a refugee in England. But in the next year Edward III, personally supporting Balliol, won the decisive battle of Halidon Hill, and the two leaders partitioned Scotland. David and his queen took refuge in France for seven years, and returned when Balliol had finally been driven from the kingdom. David tried to take advantage of King Edward III's absence in France by invading England, but seven weeks after the battle of Crécy, he was totally defeated at Neville's Cross, Durham, on October 17, 1346, and was imprisoned in England for 11 years. It was an ignominious end to a long reign which lasted 41 years.

Robert II
1371-1390

Known as Robert the Steward (Later as King Blearie, from his blood-shot eyes).

Born on March 2, 1316.
Succeeded as King of Scots on February 22, 1371 at the age of 54.
Nephew of his predecessor David, being the grandson of Robert I through his mother, Marjorie Bruce.
Married 1. in 1347 when he was 31, his mistress Elizabeth, daughter of Sir Adam Mure. She died in 1355; 2. in 1355, Euphemia, widowed Countess of Moray, daughter of the Earl of Ross. She died in 1387.
Children of Elizabeth: John (reigned as ROBERT), Walter, Robert, Alexander, Margaret, Marjorie, Elizabeth; of Isabella: David, Walter, Egidia, Catherine.
Bastards (all surnamed Stewart): John

(ancestor of the family of the Marquess of Bute), Thomas, Alexander, Sir John (of Dundonald), Sir Alexander, James, Sir John (of Cairdney), Walter.

Died at Dundonald, Ayrshire, on April 19, 1390 aged 74, having reigned 19 years. Buried at Scone.

꒰ꕤ꒱ꕤ꒱ꕤ꒱ꕤ꒱ꕤ꒱

Robert's father, Walter the Steward, was the descendant of a Breton immigrant who had been made High Steward of Scotland by David I. The office of Steward had remained in the family, and they used the surname Steward. This was spelt Stewart in Scots, and became the name of the dynasty which reigned for three centuries. Mary Queen of Scots adopted the spelling Stuart during her residence in France, in the hope that the French would pronounce the name more accurately when spelt that way. Robert the Steward was the nearest heir to the throne when David II died childless. He was old when he came to the throne, and ineffectual while he was on it. His reign was marked by a new treaty and a strong rapprochement with France.

Robert III
1390-1406

Born (and baptized JOHN) about 1337, i.e., ten years before his father's marriage.

Succeeded as King of Scots on April 19, 1390 at the age of 53.

Eldest son of his predecessor Robert.

Married in 1367 when he was 30 Annabella, daughter of Sir John Drummond. She died at Scone in 1401.

Children David, Robert, JAMES, Margaret, Mary, Elizabeth, Egidia.

Bastards (surnamed Stewart): James, Sir John.

Died of old age at Dundonald on April 4, 1406 at the age of 69, having reigned 15 years.

꒰ꕤ꒱ꕤ꒱ꕤ꒱ꕤ꒱ꕤ꒱

Since John was thought an ill-omened name for a king, John the Steward of Scotland was crowned as King Robert III. He had succeeded at about the same age as his father, and he had not the force to keep his nobles in check, nor to stop the descent of the hungry Highlanders raiding the lowlands. He maintained as Guardian (Regent) of the kingdom his brother Robert Earl of Fife, who had administered the country during his father's last years. Later he made Fife Duke of Albany but, 'being unable to govern the realm' appointed his (the king's) son David as King's Lieutenant, creating him Duke of Rothesay. These were the first dukedoms created in Scotland, and have been restricted to the Royal Family – the Prince of Wales is Duke of Rothesay now. After a disastrous invasion of Scotland by King Henry IV of England, Albany quarrelled with Rothesay, who died in suspicious circumstances. The king's sole remaining son was James, who was only 11 years old, having been born after the accession. On a voyage to

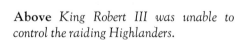

Above *King Robert III was unable to control the raiding Highlanders.*

Opposite above *Catherine Douglas is shown attempting to prevent the assassination of James I.*

Opposite below *King James I spent 18 years of his reign in captivity in the Tower of London.*

France, James was captured by the English, and the shock of this loss coincided with the death of King Robert.

James I
1406-1437

Born at Dunfermline in December 1394. **Succeeded** as King of Scots on April 4, 1406 at the age of 11 (but was a prisoner in England for the first 18 years of his reign).

Third and only surviving son of his predecessor Robert.

Married on February 2, 1424, in London, at the end of his imprisonment, when he was 29, Joan Beaufort, daughter of John Earl of Somerset and granddaughter of John of Gaunt by Katherine Swynford. She survived him and married Sir James Stewart, the Black Knight of Lorne, and died in 1445.

Children Margaret, Alexander, JAMES, Isabella, Joan, Eleanora, Mary, Annabella.

Died Assassinated in the monastery of the Preaching Friars, Perth, on February 21, 1437 at the age of 42, having reigned 30 years. He was buried at Perth, after having been taken to Rhodes.

꙳꙳꙳꙳꙳꙳꙳꙳꙳꙳꙳꙳

James began his reign from the Tower of London, and Robert Duke of Albany was appointed Governor, being succeeded on his death in 1420 by his son Murdac. The Scots, in alliance with the French, were fighting a number of battles in France against Henry V, and shared the French defeat at Agincourt. After 18 years in captivity, King James returned to Scotland resolved to re-impose law and order. One of his first demonstrations was to execute for treason the Duke of Albany, with his two sons and his father-in-law, whom he considered had not exerted himself to secure his release from the English. He next imposed an uneasy discipline on the Highlanders. His methods were ruthless, and the justice of some of his punishments were questionable. It was a revenge killing by a man with a grievance, Sir Robert Graham, that brought his death.

IACOBVS·I D·GRATIA· REX· SCOTORVM

James II
1437-1460

Known as Fiery Face

Born at Holyrood Monastery, Edinburgh, on October 16, 1430.

Succeeded as King of Scots on February 21, 1437 at the age of six.

Eldest surviving son of his predecessor James, being the younger brother of a pair of twins of whom the elder, Alexander, died in infancy.

Married at Holyrood on July 3, 1449, when he was 19, Marie, daughter of the Duke of Guelders (a lower Rhine province around Arnhem). She survived him and died in 1463.

Children JAMES, Alexander, David, John, Mary, Margaret.

Bastard John Stewart.

Died accidentally from a bursting cannon at the siege of Roxburgh on

August 3, 1460, at the age of 29, having reigned 23 years. Buried at Holyrood.

꙰꙰꙰꙰꙰꙰꙰꙰꙰꙰꙰꙰꙰

James passed his youth as titular ruler of a land in tumult with unruly lords. When he came of age, he made war on them, but could only break the power of the Earls of Douglas by treacherously killing the eighth Earl, defeating the ninth in battle, and using Parliament to decree the forfeiture of the family's estates. He then secured some order by the diversions of expeditionary wars against England, and it was at the siege of the English-held castle of Roxburgh that he died.

James III
1460-1488

Born at Stirling on July 10, 1451.
Succeeded as King of Scots on August 3, 1460 at the age of nine.
Eldest son of his predecessor James.
Married in Holyrood House on July 13, 1469 when he was 18 and she was 12, Margaret, daughter of King Christian I of Denmark, Norway and Sweden. She died in 1486.
Children JAMES, James, John.
Died murdered after battle by a soldier pretending to be a priest, at the age of 36, having reigned 27 years.
Buried at Cambuskenneth, Stirlingshire.

꙰꙰꙰꙰꙰꙰꙰꙰꙰꙰꙰꙰꙰

During his youth the Scottish lords fought, sometimes literally, for the body of the king, and James was for three years in the power of one faction. The only positive thing done by these lords not entirely for their own gain was to arrange the king's marriage with the daughter of Christian, King of Denmark, Norway and Sweden, the dowry for which was eventually agreed as the Orkneys and Shetlands and the Western Isles. After his marriage James displayed an excessive interest in male favourites, who were eventually hanged by the nobles before the king's eyes. James was always justifiably troubled by the intrigues of his two brothers, whom he imprisoned. One died and the other, Alexander Duke of

Opposite top *A groat from the reign of James II.*

Opposite middle *James III, a copy from the original at Holyrood.*

Opposite below *James III was defeated at Sauchieburn by his confederate lords.*

Right *Margaret Tudor, daughter of Henry VII, wife of James IV.*

Below *James IV was killed in battle at Flodden.*

Albany escaped and was recognized by Edward IV of England as 'King of Scotland'. The confederate lords, who had imprisoned the king for one period of two months, finally marched against James in May 1488, with the heir to the throne in their army. They defeated the king at the battle of Sauchieburn, near Bannockburn. James, who had been injured in flight from the field, was stabbed to death by a man who answered the call that a priest should attend the king.

James IV
1488-1513

Born on March 17, 1473.
Succeeded as King of Scots on June 11, 1488 at the age of 15.
Eldest son of his predecessor James.
Married at Holyrood on August 8, 1503, when he was 30 and she was 14, Margaret Tudor, eldest daughter of King Henry VII of England. She survived him, and in 1514 married Archibald Douglas, Earl of Angus, whom she divorced in 1526. But her daughter Margaret, born of this union, was the mother of Lord Darnley and grandmother of King James VI and I, making James the direct descendant of Henry VII through both his father and mother. In 1526 Margaret married Henry Stewart, Lord Methven. She died in 1541.
Children James, died 1508; a daughter, died after baptism; Arthur, died 1510; JAMES; an unnamed daughter; Alexander.
Bastards Alexander, Archbishop of St Andrews at age 12, Chancellor of Scotland at age 17, killed at Flodden at age 20; Catherine, James, Margaret, Janet.
Died Killed in battle at Flodden, Northumberland, on September 9, 1513 at the age of 40, having reigned 25 years. A disfigured body was displayed by the English victors, but not acknowledged by Scots as that of their king. The body was wrapped in lead and taken south. King James IV died when he was under sentence of excommunication by the Pope for having broken a treaty of peace with Henry VIII. Henry vainly tried to get a dis-

pensation from the Pope to bury the body, and it was left in its lead sheath above ground at the monastery at Sheen, Richmond, Surrey. Much later the head was said to have been taken home by a probing workman on the palace maintenance staff of Queen Elizabeth, and its red hair and beard were still visible. It was later buried with other bones taken from the charnel house of 'Great St Michael's' – the Church of St Michael, Wood Street, City of London. The antiquarian Stow saw the lead-wrapped body before its decapitation.

ﾷﾷﾷﾷﾷﾷﾷﾷﾷﾷﾷﾷﾷ

Over an unnerving period of 134 years in Scottish history the throne was taken successively by minors. The youngest, Mary, was seven days old. The oldest, James IV, was 15 years of age but was already accustomed to intrigue, having been brought by the rebel lords to confront his father three times, ending in the fatal battle of Sauchieburn. James developed as a competent, but rash king, imposing order with some energy on the Western Isles and Western Highlanders, but showing bad misjudgement in his policy towards England. He was duped by Perkin Warbeck, the young man who said he was a survivor of the assumed murder of the Princes in the Tower, and therefore rightful King of England.

James not only received him royally, subsidized him and married him to a kinswoman, but personally invaded England at Warbeck's side. Henry VII, preferring marriage-broking to war, tried to buy off James with the hand of his daughter Margaret. As a pageant, it was Scotland's grandest marriage, but it brought no lasting peace. James invaded England again, while Henry VIII was campaigning in France and winning the bloodless victory of the Battle of the Spurs. In a curious parallel to the almost simultaneous battles of Crécy and Neville's Cross in 1346, the Scottish leadership was virtually annihilated amid the unprecedented slaughter of the total defeat at Flodden on September 9, 1513.

James V
1513-1542

Known as the Poor Man's King

Born at Linlithgow on April 10, 1512.
Succeeded as King of Scots on September 9, 1513 at the age of 17 months.
Only surviving son (of three) of his predecessor James.
Married 1. at Notre Dame, Paris on January 1, 1537, when he was 24, Madeleine de Valois, eldest daughter of

King François I of France. She died at Holyrood on July 7, 1537; 2. by proxy in Paris in 1538, and later at St Andrews in June 1538, Marie de Guise Lorraine, daughter of the Duke of Guise Lorraine.
Children of Marie: James Duke of Rothesay, died 1541 aged ten months; Arthur Duke of Rothesay, died 1541 aged seven days; MARY.
Bastards all by different mothers, all surnamed Stewart: James I, James II Earl of Moray and Regent of Scotland, James III, Robert Earl of Orkney, John, Adam.
Died apparently in melancholia, at Falkland on December 14, 1542, aged 30, having reigned 29 years.

ﾷﾷﾷﾷﾷﾷﾷﾷﾷﾷﾷﾷﾷ

The normal turmoil among belligerent nobles exacerbated Scotland's chronic ailment, the reign of an infant king. John Duke of Albany, grandson of James II and Heir Presumptive to the throne, arrived from France, where he had been born and brought up. (He could not speak English: James IV was the last Scots King to speak Gaelic). Albany was made Governor, but there was constant friction between the French interests he represented, the English faction headed by Margaret as Queen Mother and titular Regent, and the true general interests of Scotland. Since Albany was spending twice as much time in France as in Scotland, he

128

Opposite *While Henry VIII was engaged in the Battle of Spurs, illustrated here, James IV invaded England.*

Right *Albany, governor of Scotland with Margaret, mother of the infant James V.*

Below *James V with his second wife Marie de Guise. James was known as 'The Poor Man's King'.*

IACOBVS.QVINTVS.SCOTTORVM.REX
ANNO.ÆTATIS.SVE.
Z8

MARIA.LOTHORINGIA.ILLIVS.IN.SECVNDIS.NVP
TIIS.VXOR.ANNO ÆTATIS SVE. Z 4

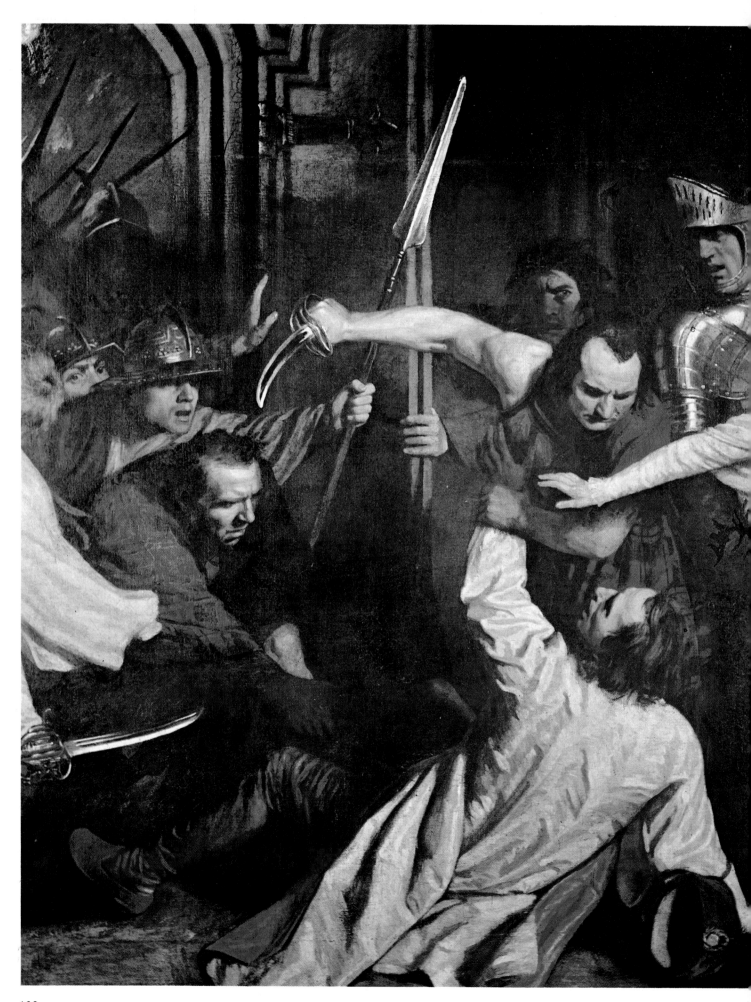

was dismissed as Governor, and James V took over full royal authority at the age of 14. He immediately associated himself with serious internecine battles (one involving 25,000 men) between warring earls, and ordered the extermination of insurgent Highland clans and border raiders. James quarrelled with King Henry VIII over Henry's ecclesiastical policy and over James's French alliance. War finally broke out, but James was disgraced when his nobles refused to accept the orders of his commander and were routed at Solway Moss. James, a sick man with no surviving legitimate children, was told of the birth of a daughter, Mary. Referring to the Stewart dynasty, which sprang from Marjorie, the daughter of Robert I, he prophesied: 'It cam' wi' a lass, and it will gang wi' a lass'. Within a week the king was dead.

Left *The death of Riccio.*

Below *Henry Stewart, Lord Darnley.*

Mary Queen of Scots 1542-1567

Born at Linlithgow on December 7, or 8, 1542.

Succeeded as Queen of Scots on December 14, 1542, aged about seven days. On the death of Mary Tudor, Queen of England, on November 17, 1558, Marie Stuart (as she then spelt her name) claimed the throne of England, asserting that Queen Elizabeth was a bastard. She and her new husband then styled themselves 'François and Marie, by the grace of God, of Scotland, England and Ireland, King and Queen'. Within a year Mary was undoubted Queen of France, through the death of Henri II and the accession of the Dauphin as King François II. He died 17 months after his accession.

Only surviving child of her predecessor James.

Married 1. in Notre Dame, Paris on April 24, 1558, when she was 15 and he was 14, François, Dauphin of France. He died, as King François II, on December 5, 1560; 2. in the chapel at Holyrood House, on July 29, 1565, when she was 22 and he was 19, Henry Stewart, Lord Darnley, eldest son of Matthew, Earl of Lennox, and his wife Margaret Douglas, daughter of Margaret Tudor by her second marriage to the Earl of Angus. Darnley, who was created Duke of Albany and styled Henry King of Scots, was murdered at Kirk of Field, Edinburgh on February 10, 1567; 3. in the chapel of Holyrood House, but according to Protestant rites, on May 15, 1567, when she was 24 and he was 31, James Hepburn, Earl of Bothwell and Duke of Orkney, eight days after Bothwell obtained a divorce from his wife Lady Jane Gordon. Mary, from imprisonment in England, obtained a divorce from him in 1570. He died insane in prison in Denmark in 1578.

Child of Darnley, JAMES.

Abdicated by constraint, in favour of her infant son on July 24, 1567, aged 24, having reigned 24 years.

Left *James Hepburn.*

131

Died executed by decapitation at Fotheringhay Castle, Northants on February 8, 1587, aged 44. Buried at Peterborough Cathedral. Later buried by her son James in King Henry VII's Chapel in Westminster Abbey.

ᖷᖷᖷᖷᖷᖷᖷᖷᖷᖷᖷᖷᖷᖷ

On Mary's accession, when she was only a week old, the regency was assigned to the next heir, James Hamilton, Earl of Arran, who was appointed Governor of the Realm and tutor to the queen. He agreed, when the child was seven months old, to Mary's betrothal to Henry VIII's son, the five-year-old Edward, later King Edward VI. The marriage was to take place when Mary was 11, and no war was to be prosecuted between England and Scotland beforehand. But, two months later, the Catholic party snatched the baby, crowned her in Stirling, repudiated the betrothal, and repealed Arran's pro-Protestant decree permitting the Bible to be read in English or Scots. In reprisal, Henry sent an invasion force which sacked Edinburgh and Holyrood and burned every village on the march south to England. He followed this with a further terroristic expedition in 1545. Scotland was now split between the escalating Protestant faction, who willy-nilly found themselves supporting an English alliance, and the Catholic party favouring the old connection with France. After the accession of the Protestant Edward VI in England, the Duke of Somerset defeated Arran at Pinkie, near Edinburgh on September 10, 1547, which was the last battle fought between the English and Scottish nations. During the subsequent English occupation, Mary went for refuge to France, where she stayed for 13 years.

The Queen Mother, Marie of Guise Lorraine, supplanted Arran as Regent (after he had, with French help, driven the English from Scotland), and administered Scotland as a French colony. The marriage of Mary Queen of Scots to the Dauphin, and his accession to the throne of France, magnified this trend. But the principles of the Protestant Reformation had spread with astonishing speed within Scotland, and the 'Lords of the (Protestant) Congregation' had already signed the First Covenant, binding themselves to make Scotland Protestant. In 1559 the return of John Knox from a sentence as a

galley-slave in France led to vandalist Protestant riots, escalating into civil war, which was ended in August 1560 by Parliamentary acceptance of the Protestant Reformation. It was in this atmosphere that Mary, now the widowed Queen of France, returned to Scotland in 1561 at the age of 18. She was charming, beautiful and brave. But she was also as rash as James IV and more passionately, irresponsibly wilful than most of the Roman emperors.

She accepted the Protestant establishment in a situation where there was a majority of Catholics among her subjects, but the new régime gratified those lords who had acquired former Church

Above *A sombre portrait of Mary, Queen of Scots, from Glasgow Museum of Art.*

Opposite top *From an old picture engraved by Vertue. It shows the surrender of Mary at Carberry Hill.*

Opposite middle *One of the famous sights in Edinburgh, John Knox's house is well-preserved.*

Opposite bottom *John Knox, founder of the most uncompromising brand of Presbyterianism in Scotland.*

James VI
1567-1625

Born in Edinburgh Castle on June 19, 1566.

Succeeded as King of Scots on July 24, 1567 at the age of 13 months. (Succeeded as King of England and Ireland on March 24, 1603 at the age of 36).

Only son of his predecessor Mary, who had abdicated and who died 20 years later.

Married at Oslo, Norway on November 24, 1589, when he was 23 and she was 15, Anne of Denmark, second daughter of King Frederick II of Denmark and Norway.

Children Henry Frederick, Prince of Wales, died 1612; Elizabeth; Margaret, died young; CHARLES; Robert and Mary and Sophia, all died young.

Died from premature old age, a quartan ague (fever with paroxysms) having developed from a chill, at his house Theobalds in Hertfordshire on March 27, 1625, aged 58, having reigned in Scotland for 57 years and in England for 22 years. Buried in King Henry VII's Chapel in Westminster Abbey.

ꗥꗥꗥꗥꗥꗥꗥꗥꗥꗥꗥ

The fate of the House of Stuart (as, in deference to Mary Queen of Scots, the name will now be spelt) offers a strong argument against hereditary monarchy, with its dismal succession of babies who were kings before they could talk. After 1567 Regents were appointed, but when the Scottish nobles were too squeamish to slaughter their infant monarch they proceeded to liquidate the Regents. Regent Moray went in 1570, the Regent Lennox in 1571, the Regent Mar died in his bed in 1572, and the Regent Morton, though he had long resigned his office, was executed in 1581 for Darnley's murder 14 years previously. By this time King James VI had assumed the government, but he was soon in 'protective custody' as a captive of the Earls of Gowrie and Mar and the Master of Glamis, who dictated all policy during the ten months for which they held him.

James's immediate reaction after escaping from this confinement was to court

property. Mary appointed as her chief minister Lord James Stewart, Earl of Moray, the illegitimate son of her father by Margaret, daughter of Lord Erskine, and he put down an early rebellion by the Catholic Earl of Huntly. As heiress to the throne of England, Mary was an inestimable prize in the European marriage market, but she impulsively married her first cousin Lord Darnley, the next in succession to the English throne after herself – and thus reinforced Elizabeth's determination not to nominate Mary as her successor to the throne. Darnley was a young libertine, and the couple were soon at odds. Within six months of the marriage Darnley engineered the murder of Mary's intimate courtier Riccio – again, in this chronicle of immaturity, an unnecessary impulsive step since Moray had already arranged that Riccio should be tried and executed. Mary was then pregnant with her only child James, who was born three months later. But by this time she was infatuated with the wild Earl of Bothwell. Bothwell, with Mary's connivance, strangled Darnley before blowing up his house, suborned a judicial trial to obtain his acquittal of murder, abducted Mary, divorced his wife, and married the queen – all in three months. One month later, Mary and Bothwell had to surrender to the army of the Lords Associators, who were determined not to accept Bothwell as king, and on July 24, 1567 Mary abdicated.

the French alliance and even dally with the acceptance of Catholicism. He was bought out of this mood by a pension of £4000 a year paid by Queen Elizabeth of England, with the assurance of advice and support in his rather glum struggle against the power groups in Scotland. The subsidy and its implication saw him through the shock of the execution of his mother, Mary Queen of Scots, in 1587, which was further mitigated by the knowledge that he was now Heir Presumptive to Elizabeth. He still had his domestic problems. James, who had spent much of his youth in scholastic study, was now developing his theory of the *Divine Right of Kings*, which was a long spring ahead of his premise that he was the Supreme Head of the Scottish Church. But even this assumption was challenged by the Scottish Reformed Church, which moved energetically to deny the authority of king or Parliament over the Church's teaching, to eradicate any hierarchy in the Church, to abolish bishops, and thus to establish Presbyterian church government, under which all ministers were of the same rank.

James temporarily accepted the establishment of Presbyterianism, but bided his time to overthrow it in favour of the Episcopal system. And it was during his preparation for this fateful reversal that he heard from a travel-sore Englishman, Sir Robert Carey, who had ridden from London to Edinburgh in 60 hours, that Queen Elizabeth was dead. King James VI of Scotland was King James I of England and Ireland.

James I of England
1603-1625

The English who welcomed the cavalcade of the new Royal Family as it made its slow, and very expensive, progression to London, saw a 37-year-old portly man of medium height with thin brown hair on his head and chin, and pale blue eyes which were popping and rolling. When he descended from his coach he showed thin legs which made him look grotesque, contrasting with his bulky thighs and trunk in even bulkier clothing; for he had his breeches and

doublet heavily quilted to make them dagger-proof. He was terrified to see drawn steel in his presence, and people said knowingly that this was because, while he was still unborn, his mother had seen his father stab her lover to death. If the king began to make this aversion clear to his new courtiers, it took some time to appreciate what he was saying, not only because of his broad Scottish speech, but because his diction was not clear, his tongue being too large for his mouth. For this reason, when he talked or drank – and he

drank heavily – there were commonly rivulets flowing from both corners of his mouth.

The English people welcomed the coming of James. It is perhaps a reflection of their vitality at that time, though it was also based on frustration arising from an international economic slump. There was no ossification of reverence then. On the death of Queen Victoria, after a reign of 63 years, the sovereign was held in such veneration that there was only sorrow at her passing, not a great joy at a new beginning. The same

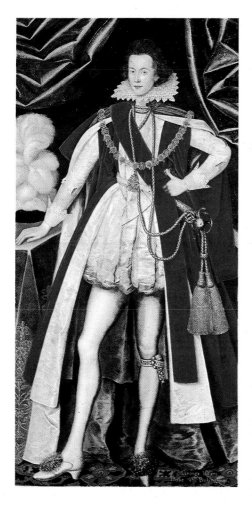

Above *George Villiers, Duke of Buckingham, favourite of James I.*

Opposite *King James I of England, latterly James VI of Scotland.*

Right *Anne of Denmark, James' wife, daughter of the King of Denmark.*

Below *James Douglas, regent of Scotland.*

is true even for the fading of poor mad George III after 60 years, though the Regency operated before his death eased the consciousness of transition. But Elizabeth, with 44 years behind her, died at a period before monarchs could mellow into lovable monuments. Intelligent people, materialistic people, wanted action. The young Elizabethans who were moved by the great series of profound and perceptive tragedies, and keenly *political* Roman plays, which were the climax of Shakespeare's work after 1600, were at one with the merchant adventurers and the restless gentry in the House of Commons in wanting to see the state transformed, a chrysalis broken, and a butterfly shimmering. But James was to prove himself a dis-

appointing butterfly.

He had developed as a good politician in Scotland, manoevring power block against power block, and even reintroducing a limited episcopacy before he left Edinburgh. But he had been dealing with a far weaker Parliament than the assembly he found in Westminster. To counter them, he chose to rule through ministers experienced in 'management'. But when the old stock of servants like the Cecils ran out, he had to rely more on more on favourites without standing, brought in from Scotland and, later, from sprigs of the aristocracy who had played no part in the rapid development of principled, individual responsibility which was the quality of this trusting age. With the last of them, George

Villiers Duke of Buckingham, there were clear grounds for assuming planned homosexual seduction on the part of the younger man. His reward – in his early twenties – was the post of chief minister and personal emoluments of some £30,000 a year in cash from the king alone, disregarding the income he was deriving from grants of land and privilege.

The reaction came from Parliament. The Commons of England, asserting the necessity for its agreement, if not control, in matters of finance and foreign policy, declared that their privileges were 'the ancient and un-doubted birthright and inheritance of the subjects of England'. James drama-tically went to Westminster, and per-sonally tore this declaration out of the Journals of the House. He had set the scene for the Civil War. His son was to inherit his hunger for absolute power, and foolishly ran rough-shod over an increasingly restless Commons.

Charles I
1625-1649

Known posthumously to the Church as Charles, King and Martyr

Born at Dunfermline on November 19, 1600.
Succeeded as King of England, Scotland and Ireland on March 27, 1625 at the age of 24.
Only surviving son of his predecessor James.
Married in June 1625, when he was 24 and she was 15, Henrietta Maria, daughter of King Henri IV of France. She survived him and died in 1669.
Children Charles, died 1629; CHARLES, born 1630; Mary; JAMES; Elizabeth; Anne; Catherine; Henry; Henrietta Anne.
Died executed by decapitation at Whitehall on January 30, 1649. Buried at Windsor.
Profile Small stature, brown eyes, brown hair with much lighter reddish facial hair, worn in a 'Van Dyck' beard with upswept moustaches. He had an impediment in his speech, though not so marked as his father's. A shy man with scrupulous personal morals, firmly religious but with a double standard in politics, not keenly intelligent, with an active appreciation of art. In childhood he was physically weak, particularly in his legs. He was a good sportsman in his youth, and later was an early devotee of horse-racing.

❧❧❧❧❧❧❧❧❧❧❧❧

Charles lived a withdrawn life as a boy, in the shadow of his manly, extrovert brother, seven years his senior, Henry Prince of Wales, who died of typhoid when Charles was 12. Later he blossomed in the warmth of attention given to him by his father's favourite,

Buckingham. In 1623 he went to Madrid with Buckingham, negotiating for his marriage to the daughter of Philip III of Spain, with the financial hope of a rich dowry. His main political aim was the restoration of Charles' sister Elizabeth and her Protestant husband Frederick V (father of Prince Rupert and grandfather of King George I) as sovereigns of the Rhine Palatinate and the kingdom of Bohemia from which they had been expelled. The mission failed, and Charles and Buckingham urged James I to declare war on Spain, a desultory hostility which did not materialize until Charles was on the throne. And then it merged into a war with France.

War demanded finance, which the Commons would not readily grant. King Charles prosecuted the war by means of arbitrary taxes and the imposition of martial law at home.

Opposite below *The well-known 'three positions' portrait of Charles I by the Flemish painter Sir Anthony Van Dyck.*

Right *The Great Seal of England under the Commonwealth.*

Below right *The execution of King Charles took place in the banqueting hall of the palace at Whitehall.*

Below *The stern founder of the Common-wealth, Oliver Cromwell. He took the title 'Lord Protector'.*

Since the Commons had been reluctant in the first Parliament of the reign to make long-term subsidies, when Charles called his second Parliament he excluded active leaders of the opposition. The third Parliament passed the *Petition of Right* which declared that arbitrary imprisonment, taxation without consent of Parliament, and the application of martial law to civilians, was illegal, together with Charles's innovations in religion. In a further session, while members held the Speaker down in his chair, the Commons passed resolutions declaring that those who either levied or paid taxes, or made religious innovations, without the authority of Parliament were enemies of the state.

Charles immediately dissolved Parliament, imprisoned the leaders of the Commons, and governed for 11 years as a dictator. The conditions for

revolt steadily matured, in the two crucial spheres of resistance to arbitrary taxation and the introduction by Archbishop Laud of a new liturgy. This saw the English (and Scottish) Churches as an organism within the Catholic Church, but more consistently faithful to first Catholic principles than any other rule – a theory which axiomatically demanded the demolition of Puritan doctrine. Scotland understandably reacted most forcibly. In 1639 the Scottish Parliament abolished episcopacy, and established an army based in northern England.

Charles was forced to call a Parliament, which impeached Archbishop Laud and the king's two able administrators Strafford and Finch. It then abolished the courts of Star Chamber and High Commission, through which Charles had imposed the sanctions of his dictatorship, and perpetuated its own life irrespective of the unsupported decision of the king. Charles was defeated in a final confrontation, the intended arrest of the Five Members, and had no alternative but a trial of arms. His adversary in charge of the Parliamentary army, was the iron-willed Oliver Cromwell. The English Parliament made a treaty of unity of aim with the Scots Parliament, and a massive Scots force was at the disposal of the left-wing movement. The ensuing Civil War tore the country apart, and sometimes drove Cromwell to cruel measures. However his personal policy in religious matters was one of tolerance.

It was to the Scottish army that, after three years of cumulative defeat, Charles surrendered in 1646. When, in the sincerity of his belief, Charles refused to approve Presbyterianism as the state religion of Scotland, the Scottish leaders handed the king over to the English Parliamentary commanders, their decision being eased by the passing of £400,000 which they claimed as back-pay. Two years of intrigue and negotiation followed. Charles was inept at the ploy of political chaffering and dissembling at which his father had excelled – but his honour kept him intransigent on any concession which touched his religious conscience or the prerogative of the Divine Right of the Lord's Appointed in which he maintained his faith. These two aspects of his character explain the Church's conception of him as a man of honour,

and Cromwell's vision of him as a man of blood. The inevitable result was the fall of the axe outside the banqueting hall of Whitehall Palace on Charles' luckless head.

Charles II
1660-1685

Born at St James's Palace, London on May 29, 1630.

Succeeded as King of England, Scotland and Ireland after the execution of his father on January 30, 1649, at the age of 19. Within a few days the Rump Parliament abolished the monarchy. But Charles was crowned King of Scotland at Scone on New Year's Day 1651. Parliament proclaimed Charles as King on May 8, 1660. He landed at Dover on May 23, and entered London on his 30th birthday, May 29, 1660.

Eldest surviving son of his predecessor Charles.

Married on May 21, 1662, when he was 31 and she was 24, Catherine of Braganza, daughter of King John IV of Portugal. She survived him and died in 1705.

No legitimate children.

Mistresses acknowledged as mothers of his children: Lucy Walters; Elizabeth Killigrew, Lady Shannon; Catherine Pegge, later Lady Green; Barbara Villiers, (Mrs Roger Palmer), later Countess of Castlemaine, later Duchess of Cleveland; Nell Gwyn; Louise de Keroualle, Duchess of Portsmouth; Moll Davies.

Bastards acknowledged by Charles: James Crofts, later Duke of Monmouth by Lucy Walters; Charlotte, Countess of Yarmouth by Elizabeth Killigrew; Charles FitzCharles, Earl of Plymouth, and Catherine, by Catherine Pegge; Anne, Countess of Sussex, Charles Fitzroy, Duke of Southampton, Henry Fitzroy, Duke of Grafton, Charlotte, Countess of Lichfield, and George Fitzroy, Duke of Northumberland by Barbara Villiers; Charles Beauclerk, Duke of St Albans, and James Beauclerk by Nell Gwyn; Charles Lennox, Duke of Richmond by Louise de Keroualle; Mary, Countess of Derwentwater by Moll Davies.

Bastard falsely ascribed Barbara

(Benedicta) Fitzroy, daughter of Barbara Villiers and John Churchill, later Duke of Marlborough.

Died after a stroke, at Whitehall Palace on February 6, 1685, at the age of 54, having reigned 24 years in Great Britain and having held the name of king for 36 years. Buried in Westminster Abbey.

Profile tall, dark complexion, black eyes, thinned moustache, profuse dark hair always worn shoulder length and as long as the wigs he adopted towards the end of his life when he grew bald. Face deeply lined early in life. Physically very fit. A dabbler in experimental science, but having the rough pragmatical experience of the 'university of life' rather than the usual courtly education. In character – alert, affectionate, garrulous, self-indulgent, cynical. Above all, a dedicated survivor. After spending 14 years out of England (apart from six weeks on the run after the battle of Worcester, and the campaign before the battle), he had, as he reminded his brother and successor, 'no wish to go on his travels again'. He played out a short-term policy of government by chicanery which just lasted his lifetime.

༝ཥ་ཥ་ཥ་ཥ་ཥ་ཥ་ཥ་ཥ་ཥ་ཥ་ཥ

From the age of 12 to 16 Charles spent his life in the camp and the field between the battle of Edgehill and his escape to France from Jersey. He spent a separate year as politician and soldier in the shameless bargaining with the Church of Scotland before the battle of Worcester – and after the adventures framing that defeat settled down through the long years of his twenties to the bored libertinism of the exiled pretender.

At his Restoration he was rapturously received by the population, more cautiously by the 'cavalier Parliament', which – after he had refused to pursue a policy of rabid vengeance against the Commonwealth regime – limited both the king's powers and his finance. Yet the Parliamentary interests decreed a war against the Dutch, the object of which was plain loot. The royal navy was inadequate, the Dutch were good fighters, and the venture was a cumulative disgrace. Charles was slowly driven to rely on King Louis XIV of France for enough finance to give him a surplus, without seriously damaging British interests by the policies which Louis expected in return – and did not noticeably get. But Parliament was growing more hostile to the king, especially in reaction to his refusal to be rigid against nonconformists to the Established Church, whether puritan dissenters or papists. With expert jockeyship Charles kept control through strong anti-Catholic protest. His brother and successor, James Duke of York, was an honest man who did not dissemble his conversion to Roman Catholicism. Charles deferred his admission to the Church until his death-bed. It was superb political timing for survival as king – but it left a situation where a more honest, less shrewd, monarch had a minimal chance of coming through. And the best that could be said in appreciation of the character of Charles' brother was that he was a brave dullard.

Opposite above *A portrait of Charles II (National Portrait Gallery).*

Opposite below *A scene from a seventeenth century coffee house.*

Left *Catherine of Braganza, wife of Charles II and daughter of John IV of Portugal.*

James II
1685-1689

Born at St James's Palace on October 15, 1633.

Succeeded as King of England, Scotland and Ireland on February 6, 1685 at the age of 51.

Younger brother of his predecessor Charles.

Married 1. at The Hague, by secret contract in August 1659, when he was 27 and she was 22, Anne Hyde, daughter of Edward Hyde, later Earl of Clarendon. Later the contract was confirmed by private marriage ceremony at her father's house in the Strand. She died in 1671; 2. by proxy on September 30, 1673, when he was 39 and she was 15, Maria Beatrice d'Este (Mary of Modena), daughter of Alfonso IV, Duke of Modena. She survived him, and died in 1718.

Children of Anne: Charles, MARY, James, ANNE, Charles, Edgar, Henrietta, Catherine; of Mary: Catherine, Isabella, Charles, Elizabeth Charlotte, JAMES (the Old Pretender), Louisa.

Mistresses Jane Middleton, Elizabeth Butler Lady Chesterfield, Goditha Price, Margaret Brook Lady Denham, Arabella Churchill, Catherine Sedley Countess of Dorchester.

Bastards among others, James FitzJames Duke of Berwick, Henry FitzJames Duke of Albemarle, and Lady Waldegrave, all by Arabella Churchill; by Catherine Sedley Countess of Dorchester, a daughter who became the wife of Sheffield Duke of Buckingham, who as a poet was the friend of Pope and as a politician was high in the councils of Queen Anne, the legitimate daughter of James II.

Left England for France (not having abdicated) on December 23, 1688 when he was aged 55 and had reigned three years. A Convention in London in January 1689 announced that he had abdicated. On February 13, 1689 William and Mary accepted the Crown.

Died at St Germain six months after a paralytic stroke on September 6, 1701, aged 67. Buried at St Germain.

Profile Tall, fair hair worn very long and later in a wig, blue eyes, graceful

Top James II foolishly tried to impose Catholicism on England.

Above Jeffreys, a severe judge aided James by his harsh sentences.

demeanour, good manners, fair intelligence, a plodding yet assiduous lecher, but uniformly dull. His mistress Catherine Sedley said of him, puzzling why she attracted him: 'It cannot be for my beauty, for he must see that I have none, and it cannot be for my wit, for he has not enough to know that I have any'. James was a professional soldier of competence who drilled himself to become an adequate professional sailor, but never could manage being a professional sovereign.

✿✿✿✿✿✿✿✿✿✿✿✿✿

James was taken prisoner at the age of 13 when Oxford surrendered during the Civil War, and he saw his father Charles I several times during the king's captivity. He escaped from St James's Palace in 1648 and was put aboard a ship sailing down the Thames – a curious anticipation of his contrived departure from the country 40 years later. He followed the army of Maréchal Turenne as an apprentice on the staff, was allowed to form a regiment with astonishing speed, and by the age of 22 was temporarily in charge of an army. In 1660 he had accepted the post of High Admiral of Spain when a rush of events made the Restoration imminent. As Lord High Admiral of England he commanded the squadron which escorted the king his brother to Dover. In the three wars with the Dutch during Charles's reign he personally acquitted himself well, in spite of some cowardice in junior ranks which lost any fruits of victory.

If Charles II held any principle as sacred and uncontestable, it was what he once described to his brother as 'the last words of your dead father, to be constant in your religion'. For this reason Charles maintained a scrupulous political loyalty to Anglicanism although by an earlier spiritual commitment he was Catholic, and by nature he was lecherous. James II, as Duke of York, was compulsively converted to Catholicism in 1668, but Charles insisted that he should still take the Anglican communion and that his surviving

Left *An anti-Catholic cartoon on the birth of the Old Pretender.*

Opposite bottom *James, Duke of Monmouth, claimant to the throne.*

children (the future monarchs Mary and Anne) should continue to be instructed as Protestants. In 1671 James announced, as openly as Charles would permit, his conversion to Roman Catholicism, and he did not shiver when the Test Act was introduced, barring him on the ground of his religion from public office and his post as Lord High Admiral. His candid attitude to his faith was such that he stood the strain of a quite unnecessary second marriage to the young Maria d'Este.

It was a step even more fateful than it seemed. It recharged the political movement which was seeking to exclude James altogether from the succession. This fervour had subsided by 1685 when, it was calculated, Mary had not conceived for four years after bearing four daughters and a son, all of whom had died. Daughters would have been no menace to the Protestant succession of Mary and Anne. But a son would be different. A son would be the immediate heir, and James's son would be a Catholic. The end of James was that finally that son was born.

James succeeded to the throne, to meet an astonishingly conciliatory Parliament and a delayed invasion by the Duke of Monmouth, Charles II's eldest and most Protestant illegitimate son, who had been canvassed as king in preference to James before the death of his father. James had ruthlessly put down this rebellion. He used regiments loaned by William of Orange, and was aided by the ferocious sentences levied by the Chief Justice, Jeffreys, with his squad of executioners. He kept as a standing army the 30,000 men whom he had concentrated for this operation. He then, with the foolish sincerity of bigotry, began to proselytize and try to suborn influential people into his faith through the bribery of office.

He simply could not find enough Catholics to supply himself with an adequate following. The unexpected, and to many fanatical Protestants incredible, birth of James's son and heir (for whom he asked the Pope to stand godfather) coincided with a state trial of Anglican bishops for sedition, based on verbal resistance to a pro-Catholic ordinance. At this stage English magnates – six moneyed lords and a bishop, not Parliament – asked William of Orange to deliver them from 'a perpetuation of evil'.

William, with an honesty equal to James's, made a public announcement that, as leading Protestant prince in Europe, he would sail to save Britain, and Louis XIV as the premier Catholic prince could make what he liked of it. After long suspense William landed in Torbay. James, advancing to meet him, was deserted by his generals, including Churchill, not yet Duke of Marlborough but brother of James's old mistress. James could not fight, and the negotiating terms of the invaders and their massing English supporters were that he should abandon Catholicism. Instead, he abandoned England for Ireland, and stayed there nearly a year and a half. He was defeated, but very carefully not killed, by the new King William at the battle of the Boyne on July 1, 1690, and was forced to retire to France. But, though he began a series of harassing operations against William, his sponsor, Louis XIV recognized reality – and the victory of the Protestant succession in Great Britain.

William III
1689-1702
Mary II
1689-1694

MARY

Born at St James's Palace on April 30, 1662.

Succeeded as Queen of England and Ireland on February 23, 1689 at the age of 26. Accepted the Crown of Scotland on May 11, 1689.

Eldest surviving daughter of her predecessor James.

Married in London on November 17, 1677, when she was 15 and he was 27, William Henry of Nassau, Prince of Orange, Stadtholder of the United Provinces (Netherlands). He survived her and died in 1702.

Children none.

Died of smallpox at Kensington Palace (which she and William had built) on December 28, 1694, aged 32, having reigned five years. Buried in King Henry VII's Chapel in Westminster Abbey.

Profile Mary was small, dark and

Top *The Duke of Cumberland decimated the last Stuart uprising at Culloden in 1746.*

Above *William and Mary at their coronation, the beginning of the Protestant succession.*

Opposite *In November 1688, William arrived at Torbay in response to a plea to save Protestantism and the constitution. The following year he and Mary were crowned joint sovereigns. Future succession was restricted to a Protestant line by an Act of Settlement.*

plump, and showed a remarkable depth of bosom for one who truly said she lived like a nun. She had been married at 15, and within a year had two miscarriages which blocked any expectation of having another child. Her husband, 12 years her senior himself in ill-health and by nature glum, was not the most sympathetic of partners. She turned to a simple religion and a humble devotion to her husband that out-shone patient Griselda's. Since he was away at the wars for eight months out of 12, she developed as a surprisingly effective Queen-in-Council.

WILLIAM

Born at The Hague on November 4, 1650.
Succeeded immediately as William III Prince of Orange, his father, William II, having died a week before his birth. Succeeded as King of England and Ireland on February 23, 1689, as King of Scotland on May 11, 1689.
Nephew of his predecessor James, being the son of James's sister Mary Stuart, Princess Royal, daughter of King Charles I.
Married Mary on November 17, 1677.
Children None.
Mistress Elizabeth Villiers, later Countess of Orkney.
Died of pleurisy at Kensington Palace, following a broken collar bone sustained when his horse stumbled over a mole-hill, on March 8, 1702, aged 51, having reigned in England 13 years. Buried in Westminster Abbey.
Profile Short and slight, with brown hair (his own when young), worn very long to the depth of the chest and dressed as carefully as a wig. Broad face, full lips, a monumentally bent nose described as 'Roman eagle'. Weak constitution and quiet disposition, but when he came to England at the age of 20 to seek the hand of Mary, King Charles II tried to drink him under the table and failed. William was the life and soul of the party. Possibly this was a sign of his political skill. William had to learn to be an expert dissembler in order to maintain the independence of the Netherlands, and, in addition, from the age of 22 to 28 he was commander-in-chief during a desperate defensive war. With all this extra-mural activity, William was not an ideal husband, especially when he knew that he would have no children from Mary and, possibly, none of his own breeding. He chose a mistress from among his wife's maids of honour, and he also had close emotional relationships with some male advisers, which his enemies inflated into sodomy. William spoke fluent English with a Dutch accent.

※※※※※※※※※※※※

William and Mary both had deprived childhoods. William never knew his father, and his mother died when he was ten. Mary's mother died when she was nine, and she was removed from intimacy with her father, James, then Duke of York, because he had declared his Catholicism and it was thought imperative that Mary should continue in the Protestant faith. Both these partners therefore craved affection, but William seems to have been unable to give it. Mary found consolation in her very uncomplicated religion, and did not stop loving her husband. It was her insistence – as the senior to her husband in her claim on the English crown – that she would resign her rights altogether to him that resulted in William and Mary being jointly offered the crown as king and queen regnant. On hearing the news that they had accepted, James II pronounced from France his solemn curse on his daughter Mary, though he continued to correspond with her sister Anne, who was the next heir.

Even accepting that James had been deposed and militarily defeated, his successor should have been by hereditary principle his infant, Catholic, son James Francis Edward. To bar this line, William and Mary, as the next heirs, accepted a Parliamentary Act of Settlement which restricted the succession to a Protestant line. The only title to the throne, therefore, was that they ruled by Act of Parliament.

Mary died too soon. William had very skilfully manipulated even the Whig politicians on whom he theoretically relied for support. But, with Mary dead, he was a more direct target for Jacobite plots. From the British point of view, he was over-busy with his insistence on hostility against France, which was more clearly in the interests of the Netherlands than of his new country. It was only in 1701, when James II died and Louis XIV recognized his son as King of England and Scotland, that politicians and patriots rallied unreservedly to support the war which William was urging. But William, too, was doomed to death. The stage was set, with Queen Anne presiding, for the soldier who had betrayed every

monarch he had had anything to do with – from Charles II, whose mistress he had pilfered to William III, who dismissed him for treasonable correspondence with James II three years after he had deserted James for William. It was the era of the Duke of Marlborough.

Anne
1702-1714

Born at St James's Palace on February 5, 1665.

Succeeded as Queen of England, Scotland and Ireland on March 18, 1702, at the age of 37. First titular Queen of Great Britain and Ireland after May 1, 1707, the date of operation of the Act of Union.

Sister-in-law of her predecessor William, sister of her predecessor Mary.

Married in the Chapel Royal on July 28, 1683, when she was 18 and he was 30, Prince George of Denmark, brother of King Christian V. He died in 1708.

Children (excluding nine still-born): Mary, died 1687; Anne Sophia, died 1687; William Duke of Gloucester, 1689-1700; Mary, died 1690; George, died 1692.

Died at Kensington Palace, two days after an apoplectic fit, on August 1, 1714, aged 49, having reigned 12 years. Buried in Westminster Abbey.

Profile Medium height, stout, dark hair, high colour yielding later to a fiery red face. A strong Anglican, but neither intelligent nor accomplished.

ﻬﻬﻬﻬﻬﻬﻬﻬﻬﻬﻬﻬﻬ

The central arena of Anne's life was her marriage to George of Denmark, a kindly nincompoop of whom Charles II reported: 'I have tried him drunk and tried him sober, and either way there is nothing in him'. George, a constant man, gave Anne 17 pregnancies, but because of a constitutional defect only five children were born alive and only one survived for an appreciable time, dying at 11. During her enforced domesticity, Anne made an intimate of Sarah Churchill, whose husband, later

Opposite above *Blenhein Palace, Queen Anne's gift to the Churchill family for Marlborough's victories.*

Opposite below *George I, 'a likeable, ridiculous king'. Responsibility for State was given to Walpole.*

Left *The Duke of Marlborough. His manipulation of power was often based on deceit.*

Below *A painting of Queen Anne from the National Portrait Gallery. Her intimate friend was Sarah Churchill.*

KING GEORGE

Earl and later Duke of Marlborough, was the guiding political influence in her life until they quarrelled irrevocably in 1711. Churchill handled Anne's acceptance of William and Mary as successors to her father, James II, but involved Anne in his own disgrace when William sent him to the Tower for conducting correspondence with the exiled Jacobite Court. He emerged, and changed his tune. The death of Anne's only heir, the young Duke of Gloucester, in 1700 increased the danger of a Jacobite succession, and the Act of Settlement was amended to secure the crown to the Protestant Hanoverians after the death of Anne.

In the diversion of the long and mainly victorious war against the French, Marlborough worked mainly for the ascendant Whigs. But throughout Anne's reign there was no certainty that the queen herself would not engineer a Jacobite succession. It was only over her dying body, after she had collapsed with apoplexy at an angry Privy Council meeting, that the Whigs mustered their strength to force their leader into office. The Whigs fulfilled the lawful Act of Settlement and called in George, Elector of Hanover to assume the British crown. It was an accession no longer dependent on separate assent by Scotland, for the Scottish Parliament had been dissolved by the Act of Union in 1707. Parallel with this Act there was passed the Act of Security, which guaranteed the permanence of the Presbyterian rule, which William III had reintroduced, as the State Church of Scotland.

George I
1714-1727

Born at Hanover on March 28, 1660.
Succeeded as Elector of Hanover in 1698, as Duke of Zell in 1700, as King of Great Britain and Ireland on August 1, 1714 at the age of 54.
Second cousin of his predecessor Anne, both being great-grandchildren of King James VI & I. George was the son of Sophia Electress of Hanover, who was the daughter of Elizabeth, sister of Charles I and James II and wife of

Frederick, Elector Palatine and titular King of Bohemia.

Married in November 1682, when he was 22 and she was 15, Sophia Dorothea, daughter of the Duke of Brunswick. He divorced her in 1694, after the violent death of her lover, and she died in 1726 at the end of a 32-year imprisonment.

Children GEORGE, Sophia Dorothea.

Mistresses among many, Ehrengard de Schulenberg, later Duchess of Kendal; Charlotte de Kielmanssegge, later Countess of Darlington; Mrs Anne Brett; the Duchess of Shrewsbury.

Bastards Lady Walsingham by Schulenberg; Lady Howe by Kielmanssegge.

Died near Osnabrück after a paralytic stroke caused by indigestion from melons consumed when he was not sufficiently recovered from sea-sickness, on June 12, 1727, at the age of 67, having reigned in England 12 years.

Profile Short, pale-faced, bulbous blue eyes, clean-shaven and with his head shaven for a wig. A military man with simple tastes for country sport and fat women – though his principle mistress, aged 60 on his accession, was a tall bag of bones. Lady Mary Montagu called him: 'An honest blockhead . . . more properly dull than lazy'. He never spoke English, but in public life in England spoke more French than German.

❦❦❦❦❦❦❦❦❦❦❦❦

The death of Anne ended the reign of the House of Stuart, though the descendants of James II lived on to invade Great Britain in 1715 and 1745. James IV's prediction, 'It cam' wi' a lass, it will gang wi' a lass' was true, but with a different woman, a century and a half later. The surname of the British Royal Family was now Guelph. This was an Italianized form of the German Welf, which gained its notoriety in the struggle between the Guelphs and Ghibellines (the houses of Welf and Waiblingen). The Guelph who qualified for the throne of Great Britain was the mainly comic George I. George was a minor German prince who spent his younger life soldiering and wenching, leaving his wife to stay at home and cuckold him, apparently out of temperament as well as boredom. When Charlotte de Kielmanssegge, the fairer and fatter of the two permanent mistresses whom George kept in his harem, reported an indiscretion of

Above *Princess Sophia, Electress of Hanover and mother of George I. She was descended from Charles I.*

Opposite *An engraving of George II, who was strongly influenced by his queen, Caroline of Anspach.*

Sophia's with a Swedish Count von Königsmarck, a certain conspiracy was hatched. The count was given a false assignation with Sophia, from which he never returned: but his bones were found under her dressing-room floor-boards 20 years later. Meanwhile Sophia was divorced and imprisoned in a castle, where she died after 32 years. Twenty years after the scandal, George succeeded to the throne of Great Britain – and brought Charlotte de Kielmanssegge with him. George spoke no English, and the lady, who thought she knew the language, would have done better to have kept her mouth shut. When the harem was mobbed on its arrival in London, she leaned out of the coach window and, attempting to ingratiate herself with the mob, declared: 'You mistake, my friends. We come here for your goods'. The seraglio then settled down in St James's Palace to take what bribes were offered for the lucrative offices of state which stood vacant.

As a Hanoverian in England – from which he escaped whenever he could – George I was a likeable, ridiculous king. It did not matter. It was even an advantage. He left the business of government to his ministers, and the great manager, Sir Robert Walpole, came into power. There was an awkward gap when he resigned on one point of principle, but he had to be recalled for stability when the country shuddered with the bursting of the South Sea Bubble, a broad-based speculative company swindle in which the king's mistresses were involved. From that time on, even though the morality of the time allowed gigantic political corruption, modern Parliamentary government based on Cabinet responsibility began to be shaped.

George II
1727-1760

Born at Herrenhausern, Hanover on November 10, 1683.
Succeeded as King of Great Britain and Ireland, and Elector of Hanover on June 12, 1727.
Only son of his predecessor George.
Married in 1705 when he was 21 and she was 22, Caroline of Anspach, daughter of John, Margrave of Brandenburg-Anspach. She died in 1737.
Children Frederick, Anne, Amelia, Caroline, George, William, Mary, Louisa.
Mistresses among others, Henrietta Howard, later Countess of Suffolk; Madame von Walmoden, later Countess of Yarmouth; Lady Deloraine.
Died at Kensington Palace from a burst blood vessel on October 25, 1760, aged 76, having reigned 32 years. Buried in Westminster Abbey.
Profile Short, fair, red-faced, with popping blue eyes. Military-minded and very orderly – he always visited one of his mistresses at nine o'clock, sometimes standing, watch in hand, waiting for the precise moment. He was the sincerely appreciative patron of the composer Handel, whom his father had restored to favour when he came to England. He had little other refinement. He talked English with a German accent, and used to declare: 'I hate bainting and boetry'.

᭢᭢᭢᭢᭢᭢᭢᭢᭢᭢᭢᭢᭢

As Prince of Wales, George II had been on bad terms with his father and had been the centre of Tory intrigue against the standing Whig Government. Walpole, George I's Prime Minister, had done much to defuse the explosiveness, but expected to be dismissed on the accession of the son. When Walpole had to tell him of his father's death, George II did indeed make the preliminary motions of appointing a new adviser. But the new Queen Caroline skilfully persuaded him to change his mind, on the understanding that Walpole would put through for them a much higher income than they expected. Caroline did indeed cosset and manage her husband, and Walpole stayed in

office until long after her death. George II had been a soldier all his youth, had served under Marlborough at Oudenarde and, at the age of 60, was to command the English and Hanovarian forces which won the battle of Dettingen. He could therefore be excused a military strut to his walk. But the popular rhyme went:

'You may strut, dapper George, but 'twill all be in vain,
We know 'tis Queen Caroline, not you, that reign'.

Though George II was publicly unfaithful to Caroline, the pair were also publicly and absurdly amorous, and the queen's death was a severe shock. As she was dying, she begged him to marry again. 'No, no, I shall take mistresses', he said in tears. 'Good God', said the queen, 'marriage doesn't bar mistresses'. But her death was a blow for Walpole, too, and it coincided with the beginning of his decline. He had kept Great Britain at peace through a generation, but now the king was ambitious for war – against the usual enemies, France and Spain – and others of his ministers did not dissuade him. But by 1745 George had to speed home from Europe to tackle the serious Jacobite invasion of the Young Pretender, Bonnie Prince Charlie. The situation became critical, but the tide of Charles's southward march was eventually turned, and George's younger brother, the Duke of Cumberland, won the decision at Culloden – and earned the title 'Butcher' from his ruthless reprisals afterwards. The country went back to war, gaining massive imperial victories which closed the reign.

George III
1760-1820

Known in his middle years as Farmer George

Born at Norfolk House, St James's Square, on June 4, 1738. Norfolk House was the residence of his father, Frederick Prince of Wales, who was on bad terms with King George II and did not reside in a palace.

Succeeded as King of Great Britain, King of Ireland and Elector of Hanover on October 25, 1760 at the age of 22.

Above *George III.*

Opposite *Bonnie Prince Charlie, last Stuart Pretender to the English throne.*

The titularly separate kingdom of Ireland was incorporated with Great Britain by the Act of Union of 1801, after which George was styled King of Great Britain and Ireland. Under an article of the Treaty of Amiens, 1802, George and his successors formally renounced the style, which they had always claimed in official proclamations, of 'King of France'. He abandoned this at a time when France was not a monarchy, but in 1804 Napoleon proclaimed himself as Emperor of the French. After 1815 Hanover, which had been conquered and absorbed by Napoleon, was freed and declared a kingdom, and George III became King of Hanover, followed by his successors George IV and William IV. Since the Salic Law, forbidding female succession,

operated in Hanover, Queen Victoria did not succeed and the kingdom passed to her uncle Ernest, Duke of Cumberland. Hanover was extinguished by incorporation with Prussia after siding with Austria in the war of 1866. It is now part of Lower Saxony, in the German Federal Republic. While British kings reigned over Hanover (which was little more than the English nickname for the territory) the land was officially called in English Brunswick-Lüneburg. Ironically, it was on Lüneberg Heath that England's Field Marshal Montgomery imposed the surrender of German arms to end the war in 1945.

Grandson of his predecessor George, being eldest son of Frederick Prince of Wales and his wife, Augusta of Saxe-Gotha. He died in 1751, she died in 1772.

Married at St James's Palace on September 8, 1761, when he was 23 and she was 18, Charlotte Sophia, daughter of the Duke of Mecklenburg-Strelitz. She died in 1818.

Children GEORGE Prince Regent and King; Frederick Duke of York, WILLIAM Duke of Clarence, Charlotte, Edward Duke of Kent, Augusta, Elizabeth, Ernest Duke of Cumberland, Augustus Duke of Sussex, Adolphus Duke of Cambridge, Mary, Sophia, Octavius, Alfred, Amelia.

Died of old age at Windsor on January 29, 1820 at the age of 81, having reigned 59 years. Buried in St George's Chapel, Windsor.

Profile Tall, fair, fresh complexion, clean-shaven, with the Guelph bulbous blue eyes. Very devoted to exercise and a meagre diet for self-discipline. An accomplished musician and a very keen collector of books and prints. His domestic interest was always in the technique of agriculture. He was a hard worker to the point of breakdown. In later life he appealed to many of his subjects of his expertise in farming, but he had already struck a responsive chord in his first public utterance as king: 'Born and educated in this country, I glory in the name of Briton'. He was sensual, moral and methodically pious. A very fast developer after an extremely slow intellectual start, he became increasingly, almost paranoically, autocratic in his judgements. In his last years of madness he was a remote, senile creature who did little but play on his harp.

༺ఌఌఌఌఌఌఌఌఌఌ༻

King George III came to the throne as a timorous youth of 22, only recently aware after a backward childhood that he had any intellectual grasp, and tormented by an immediate problem: he was anxious to surround himself with ministers of moral standing, yet he was half fearful that his former tutor, the Earl of Bute, whom he was appointing as Prime Minister, was his mother's lover. In a dramatic change of character after his accession, he swiftly acquired both confidence and obstinacy, and set out boldly to obtain four objectives. He would claw back for the crown its old royal prerogative; he would smash the ruling Whig oligarchy; he would end what he called the 'bloody and expensive' Seven Years War; and he would campaign vigorously throughout Britain against 'vice, profaneness and immorality'. He promptly instituted a regular prayer meeting for his Council in the draughty corridors of Windsor Castle.

The gifted profligate politician and propagandist John Wilkes – who, as he himself said, 'became a Patriot by accident' – developed as an antagonist opposed to the king on every front, and powerfully supported by the Whig aristocrats. Wilkes challenged the king and his corrupt advisers by publishing the historic No. 45 of his journal *The North Briton*, which attacked the 'dishonourable' peace and its ratification by means of the king's bribery. The king decided that this noxious spearhead of opposition should be liquidated in a manner exemplary to the rest of the British Press, by imprisonment and persecution under an arrest warrant which was later declared illegal. Wilkes's resistance became the focus of extraordinary popular support on the platform of personal liberty for the politically powerless lower classes of Great Britain.

Wilkes's prolonged resistance also excited deep sympathy among the colonists of North America, on whom George III had turned a baleful eye, resolving that the wilfulness of these upstarts must be curbed. He pushed through the Stamp Act, which provoked eloquent protests among the Americans against the principle of being taxed without being represented in Parliament. The Americans then developed revolutionary concepts of 'essential rights, rights founded in the law of God and nature' which were superior to those held by George III under any form of political constitution. The alert king swiftly recognized this opposition as a fundamental challenge. He over-reacted to the skilful American propaganda. He took it as a personal affront and increased the intensity of a personal, and already almost manic, feud against the Americans until it could be reliably reported: 'The king hates most cordially every American because he thinks they have an attachment to their Liberty'.

George began the political build-up within Britain, increasing his personal power against his supposed servants, the accredited ministers, by intensifying the bribery by which he supported the servile opposition known as the King's Friends. This culminated in his assumption of almost absolute power in 1770, the bludgeoning of America with four punitive Acts of Parliament against Massachusetts and Boston which incited armed resistance, and the final recourse to a state of war. George entered the war with an inflexible aim of insisting on an unconditional surrender by the colonists. He would allow no minister to take office until the man had signed a declaration 'that he is resolved to keep the empire entire, and that no troops shall consequently be withdrawn from America, nor independence *ever* allowed'. This inability to consider concessions was political madness. Faced with military defeat, he prolonged the war by blockade and devastation, and saw what he had intended as a backyard struggle for family discipline develop into a war against the Great Powers, France, Spain, Holland and the Northern Alliance – the precise situation which he had been trying to deflate when he came to the throne.

He lost America, and revolutionized Great Britain, because his concept of strong paternal patriotism ran counter to the vital causes of the age: personal liberty and colonial liberty. Yet, in his final madness, he may have been comforted by the realization that some of the things he originally fought for

had been achieved. He *had* purged the political life of the country, even though the process had called dangerous demagogy into action, by smashing the increasingly self-centred corruption of the Whig reigning families. He had not avoided war, but he had pulled the country out of the internal weakness brought by the Seven Years War, and had set Britain on a course of stable (if finally brittle) government which at least sailed her through the hurricane of the French Revolution and on to Trafalgar and Waterloo.

George IV
1820-1830

Known as Prinny

Born in St James's Palace on August 12, 1762

Succeeded as King of Great Britain and Ireland and King of Hanover on January 29, 1820 at the age of 57, having been Regent since February 1811.

Eldest son of his predecessor George.

Married in December 1785, when he was 23 and she was 29, Maria Fitzherbert, née Smythe, a twice-widowed Roman Catholic. This union was not valid according to the Royal Marriages Act of 1772, which decreed that the king must consent to all marriages of possible heirs and that they must conform to the Act of Succession. George repudiated this marriage, swearing that it had not taken place, in 1795 when it became necessary for him to make an approved marriage in order to get his debts paid. But the relationship continued until 1803. She died in 1837.

Married formally in early 1795, when he was 32 and she was 26, Caroline Amelia Elizabeth, daughter of Charles Duke of Brunswick and Augusta, elder sister of George's father, George III. They separated in 1796 and she died in 1821.

Child of Caroline, Charlotte.

Mistresses Mary Robinson (Perdita), Lady Jersey, Lady Hertford, Lady Conyngham, and some 14 others.

Died at Windsor of the effect of obesity on the heart, suffering from dropsy, gout, gall stones and blindness, and over-dosed with laudanum, on June 25, 1830 at the age of 67, having reigned

Opposite *George Washington, leader of the colonist revolt against England, became the first American president.*

Above *Queen Charlotte, wife of George III. Their marriage ceremony took place at the palace at St. James, September 8, 1761.*

151

ten years. Buried in St George's Chapel, Windsor.

Profile Tall, florid, always at least plump, with curly brown hair and fine eyes. Clean-shaven, with a strong chin and a fine face. He was extremely sociable, witty and a good mimic. He had more than a veneer of culture and was a connoisseur of art and furniture. He was also a vain, unreliable and often obscene rake. His reputation for honour was tarnished on the state level by his straight lie about his relationship with Mrs Fitzherbert to Charles James Fox, who had undertaken the task of persuading Parliament to set his affairs right, and on the social level by the fact that as a racehorse-owner he had to be warned off the course at Newmarket.

George IV debased the image of British monarchy to a level never reached before, using his position merely as the instrument of living in self-indulgence. If he had had that power of political murder which he envied in Henry VIII he might well have used it, but his only positive political action was reaction, particularly the blocking of political concessions to Roman Catholics. His life provided the strongest pragmatical argument against the principal of hereditary sovereignty, and British culture could only be contaminated by his label of The First Gentleman in Europe.

Opposite *A cartoon by Gilray of George IV, mocks his enforced marriage to Caroline. His first marriage to Maria Fitz-Herbert was not recognized as valid and was annulled.*

Below *Buckingham Palace, home of the Royal Family was built by George IV when he was Prince Regent on the site of Buckingham House.*

William IV
1830-1837

Known as The Royal Tar, The Sailor King

Born at Buckingham Palace on August 21, 1765.

Succeeded as King of Great Britain and Ireland, King of Hanover, on June 25, 1830.

Eldest surviving brother of his predecessor George, Frederick Duke of York having died in 1827.

Married at Kew on July 13, 1818, when he was 52 and she was 25, Adelaide, daughter of the Grand Duke of Saxe-Meiningen. She survived him and died in 1849.

Children Charlotte, Elizabeth, both died shortly after birth.

Mistresses Mrs Wentworth, Sally Winne, Mrs Dorothy Jordan, née Bland, (1790–1811).

Bastards (All the children of Mrs Jordan, and all surnamed FitzClarence) George, Henry, Sophia Lady de L'Isle and Dudley, Mary, Frederick, Elizabeth Countess of Erroll, Adolphus, Augusta Lady Gordon, Augustus, Amelia Lady Falkland.

Died at Windsor of a circulatory disorder aggravated by asthma on June 20, 1837, aged 71, having reigned seven years less five days. Buried in St. George's Chapel, Windsor.

Profile Burly, blue-eyed, bluff. Cropped red hair, clean-shaven. As king, 'a little old, red-nosed, weather-beaten, jolly-looking person, with an ungraceful air and carriage'. Washington Irving said: 'His Majesty has an easy and natural way of wiping his nose with the back of his forefinger which, I fancy, is a relic of his middy habits'. A simple sailor, very garrulous, who recognized his limitations and did the best he could in the unexpected station to which he had been called.

కికికికికికికికికికికికి

William had been, between the ages of 12 and 24, a professional sailor, not of

great brilliance though he commanded three ships and emerged as a young rear-admiral. (Nelson, at whose wedding William presided, had to wait until he was 39 before attaining this rank). But after 1789 William never went to sea, except in his rank as sole Admiral of the Fleet, commanding it for a royal inspection. In 1790 he met Mrs Jordan, the stage name of a popular Irish actress born Dorothy Bland, who had previously had a varied and not always secure love-life. They settled down quietly together in Bushy Park, Hampton Court, where William had the Ranger's Lodge, and Mrs Jordan bore him ten children, all brought up in serene domesticity until they displayed the aggression of adolescence – a presage of much deeper insolence in later life. William had an inadequate allowance from the State, and when his debts were heavy, Mrs Jordan used to put on her grease-paint again for a stage tour which, because of her talent, could bring in some thousands of pounds.

Because William accepted this arrangement, it is difficult not to censure him for his final exclusion of Mrs Jordan. But it seems to have been done because of the death of love rather than a questing lust, and William never abandoned the children. After 20 years William pensioned off Mrs Jordan, and began to seek a rich bride in order to support their children. The search took seven years, during which Dorothy died in misery. By this time William was third in succession to the throne. The eventual bride, however, Princess Adelaide of Saxe-Meiningen, brought no dowry save a warm heart and the assurance that she would cherish William's bastards. She loved him well, welcomed the FitzClarences, even when they were insulting, and bore her own children to William – though fewer than he conceived: she miscarried several times, and her longest surviving child lived only four months. She endured all this with sweetness. She told the Duchess of Kent, mother of the Victoria who was eventually to succeed her husband: 'My children are dead, but your child lives, and she is mine too'.

In 1827 the death of the Duke of York made William heir to the throne, and in 1830 he took it with his natural affability and lack of hypocrisy, chatting about the total of game the mourners

had bagged before making his obituary speech at George IV's funeral, and nodding to his friends as he moved up the aisle for his coronation. He was 65 years old, and nobody asked much of him except to be different from his hated brother who had died. But, with his good sense of duty, he did one thing which created a historic and binding precedent on the future of constitutional monarchy in Great Britain. He was old-fashioned, perhaps reactionary. But when the Whig Government was returned to power pledged to introduce the Great Reform Bill, he respected their mandate, jibbed at their intransigence, but ultimately consented to Lord Grey's request that he should, if necessary, create enough new Whig peers to force the measure through the Tory House of Lords if the Commons showed that they overwhelmingly desired the Reform. Because he openly accepted this necessity, then persuaded the Tories not to force its use, he advanced democratic government by more than a stumble, and pointed out the course of duty to a no less diehard Sailor King, George V in 1911.

Victoria
1837-1901

Born in Kensington Palace on May 24, 1819.

Succeeded as Queen of Great Britain and Ireland on June 20, 1837 at the age of 18. The kingdom of Hanover passed to her uncle Ernest, Duke of Cumberland. She was proclaimed as Empress of India in 1877.

Niece of her predecessor William, being only daughter of his deceased younger brother, Edward Duke of Kent.

Married at the Chapel Royal, St James's Palace on February 10, 1840, when both were 20, Albert, Prince of Saxe-Coburg-Gotha. He died in 1861.

Children Victoria, Princess Royal, later Queen of Prussia and Empress of Germany, died 1901; EDWARD, Prince of Wales; Alice, Grand Duchess of Hesse, died 1892; Alfred, Duke of Edinburgh and Duke of Saxe-Coburg-Gotha, died 1899; Helena, Princess of Schleswig-Holstein, died 1923; Louise, Duchess of Argyll, died 1914; Arthur, Duke of Connaught, died 1942; Leopold, Duke of Albany, died 1884; Beatrice, Princess of Battenberg, died 1944.

Died at Osborne, Isle of Wight of old age – brain failing, life slowly ebbing – on January 22, 1901 at the age of 81, having reigned 63 years. Buried at Frogmore, Windsor.

Profile Very short (5ft), fair hair, blue eyes, not a striking beauty but very proud of her neck and shoulders. Her sense of duty overcame her sense of fun at an early age, and she soon became the worried, masterful manager, censor of details, prolific mother and, later, penny-plain theatrical widow of popular appraisal. In the arts, although she was fond of the simpler contemporary music, her only real sensitivity was with writers, and she was an effective sentimental writer herself.

❧❧❧❧❧❧❧❧❧❧❧❧❧

Positive family planning was the only motive which contributed to the birth of Victoria. In 1817 Charlotte, the only daughter of the Prince Regent who was afterwards George IV, died in childbirth. George, aged 55 and rotten with debauchery, now had no direct heirs. The throne must go down the line of his younger brothers. But *they* had no heirs. Mad King George was near his death. But of his mighty brood of 15 children, though 12 survived, the five princesses had never had a child between them, and the seven princes, though boasting many a bastard, had not one legitimate offspring.

Four of these princes, all of them royal dukes, had never bothered to marry. An official call went out to them to remedy the situation at this late hour and produce an heir to the throne. It was Parliament which made this appeal, and Parliament offered a substantial reward for acquiescence: a vastly increased income allocated im-

Below *Queen Victoria with the infant Duke of Connaught on the terrace at Osborne House.*

Opposite *A severe, dignified portrait of the aged Queen.*

mediately on marriage, and the discreet settlement of the royal duke's individually heavy debts. William Duke of Clarence, aged 52, Edward Duke of Kent, aged 50, and Adolphus Duke of Cambridge, aged 43, responded to the call with prompt loyalty. Augustus Duke of Sussex, aged 44, had made, and regretted, one morganatic marriage; but he was too honourable to repudiate it as his eldest brother George had done; and in any case he was living comfortably in morganatic sin with Lady Cecilia Underwood (with whom Queen Victoria later sanctioned a morganatic marriage once Augustus's first morganatic wife had died, and Cecilia became Duchess of Inverness).

William had abandoned Mrs Jordan, and was free to propose himself to Adelaide of Saxe-Meiningen. Edward had a harsher problem. He had lived for 27 years with a French lady, Julie de St Laurent, taking her abroad on his military appointments to the West Indies, Canada and Gibraltar, and later sharing with her his comparatively penurious life in England. Madame de St Laurent, a mild and affectionate woman, literally had convulsions when

she read in the newspaper the public exhortation of her lover to marry. But Edward, a double-dealer, had already made a provisional proposal to a German widow, Victoria of Saxe-Coburg, Princess of Leiningen.

The third runner, Adolphus Duke of Cambridge, dashed from behind and was married before his brothers, taking Princess Augusta of Hesse-Cassel. Edward of Kent swiftly consigned Julie de St Laurent into a French convent, and announced his engagement to Victoria. William of Clarence grabbed Adelaide of Saxe-Meiningen, and William and Edward were married on the same day, July 13, 1818, at the same place, Kew Palace, the wedding service being printed in English and German for the benefit of the brides.

The country, gratified by the loyal response of its princes, now awaited announcements of pregnancy. Cambridge led, and in March 1819 produced George. In the same month Clarence's poor wife Adelaide bore a premature girl who did not live, and, as has been said, the Clarences, after many hopes, were eventually childless. Kent's wife Victoria had a daughter in May

1819, and since Kent was senior to Cambridge, young George was edged out of the succession as long as the daughter lived. The daughter lived 81 years, 63 of them as Queen Victoria. (Young George, second Duke of Cambridge, became a controversial Field-Marshal and Commander-in-Chief to Victoria, married an actress morganatically. He produced three Fitz Georges, and died three years after Victoria in 1904).

The new Kent baby was to be called Georgina after the Prince Regent, and Alexandrina after the Czar of Russia, her other godfather, whom the Prince Regent detested. In an amazing scene at the christening, the Prince Regent refused to name her Georgina, struck out two other names suggested at the font, and contemptuously said the child could be called Victoria after her mother. Seven months later, little Victoria's father, the Duke of Kent, was dead of pneumonia. His own father, George III, had died six days earlier and they were buried together. George IV was king, William IV was to follow him, and if he still had no living children the way was set for the eventual

succession of Queen Victoria.

She came to the throne in 1837, less than a month after attaining her majority, which freed the nation of a Regency conducted by her mother the Duchess of Kent, who was universally regarded as odious. William IV had had little time or influence to cleanse the Court, and Victoria's first years as queen were also dogged by unnecessary scandal. But she married Albert in 1840, and settled down to battle for the dignity of British royalty. It was not an easy struggle. She and Albert, and later their wayward son Edward, endured periods of intense unpopularity. But her invincible knack of survival, her undoubted principles of morality, and her gradual suppression (though not extinction) of her own autocratic temperament, all running parallel with an active era of economic and imperial aggrandizement, laid fresh foundations for the acceptance of a new-model constitutional monarchy. Victoria was the 'Grandmother of Europe' through the marriages of her numerous family into every royal house. Within a generation of her death this regality had all been washed away into republicanism or communism. Her own imperial dominion has shattered since. But republicanism in Great Britain is weaker now than it was in the last decade of her life.

Opposite *Victoria's coronation. Her accession to the throne was dogged with indignity and scandal.*

Below *Victoria is shown here arriving to lay the foundation stone of the Victoria and Albert Museum.*

Edward VII
1901-1910

Known as the Peace-Maker

Born at Buckingham Palace on November 9, 1841.

Succeeded as King of Great Britain and Ireland, and Emperor of India, on January 22, 1901, aged 59.

Eldest son of his predecessor Victoria.

Married at St George's Chapel, Windsor on March 10, 1863, when he was 21 and she was 18, Alexandra, daughter of King Christian IX of Denmark. She survived him and died in 1925.

Children Albert, Duke of Clarence, died 1892; GEORGE; Louise, Duchess of Fife, died 1931; Victoria, died 1935; Maud, Queen of Norway, died 1938; John, died 1871.

Mistresses Nellie Clifden, Hortense Schneider, Princesse Jeanne de Sagan; Harriet, Lady Mordaunt (by her affirmation), Miss Chamberlayne, actress Lily Langtry, Patsy Cornwallis-West, Sarah Bernhardt, Daisy Brooke Lady Warwick, La Goulue, Georgiana Countess of Dudley, Mrs Alice Keppel, Agnes Keyser.

Bastards Paternity by Edward VII was claimed by many of the children themselves concerned; but Edward had long liaisons only with women who had complaisant living husbands, and he officially acknowledged no natural children, though he was unnaturally kind to some.

Died at Buckingham Palace of pneumonia and a series of heart attacks on May 6, 1910, aged 68, having reigned nine years. Buried in St George's Chapel, Windsor.

Profile 5ft 4in high, blue eyes, strong nose, receding chin covered permanently from the time of his twenties by a full beard. His speech was seductive. An American journalist wrote: 'He possesses

Opposite *Three generations are shown here; Victoria, the future King Edward VII and his wife Alexandra, and the young Duke of Windsor grandson of Edward and son of the future George V.*

Left *Edward VII with Alexandra. His wife tolerated his numerous mistresses.*

one of the clearest, fullest and best modulated voices I have ever heard, and its sympathetic tones excite a magnetic influence on the hearer'. But he always gave the 'R' sound an indistinct German burr. Self-indulgent with women and food, he quickly became corpulent and acquired the nickname 'Tum-tum.' He had great charm, but allowed intimacy only on his own terms, crushing any reciprocation of his informal advances. He had no affinity with literature, but he was a good linguist and a devotee of the theatre – including the French theatre – and was for long an enthusiast of the music hall.

⁎⁎⁎⁎⁎⁎⁎⁎⁎⁎⁎⁎⁎⁎

Edward was christened Albert Edward and called Bertie by his family. But on his succession he announced that he would be called Edward VII, tactfully explaining that there could be only one Albert, 'who by universal consent is, I think deservedly, known by the name of Albert the Good'. Edward was brought up with strict severity as 'a vicarious atonement for the wickedness of George IV'. But there were many moments in his later life when he was publicly compared with the profligate Prince Regent. His mother had a physical aversion to him for a long time after the death of his father when Edward was 20 – which Victoria wrongly attributed to Albert's collapse at the disclosure that Edward had recently had an affair with an actress. Edward was barred from exerting any political influence for 40 years, and he bitterly resented this, particularly in the field of foreign policy.

Here his extensive family contacts in Europe, and his easy sociability which was in marked contrast to his mother's withdrawn isolation, gave him, he considered, an expertise which was neglected. In consequence, he devoted himself to a life of personal indulgence, which was not diminished in debauchery by the cover of social grace and exquisite manners under which it was carried out. His wife Alexandra, a not very intelligent woman but both sensitive and loyal, was compelled to acquiesce in his amours with the dignity which she could well muster. Edward was in financial difficulties during the middle of his life, but was finally made solvent with the help of able investment advisers and the good fortune of being a successful race-horse owner. He made £415,840 from racing in his last 24 years.

When Edward came tardily to the throne he was active in changing a traditional British alignment in foreign policy. He gained the goodwill of France and began not only foreign alliances but also active rearmament against the military aggrandizement of Germany under Kaiser Wilhelm, a nephew of Edward whom he thoroughly detested. At home, as a true Tory like

Below *One of Edward's mistresses was the actress Lily Langtry. She is shown here dressed for Cleopatra.*

Opposite *The official coronation invitation showing Edward VII and Alexandra.*

162

KING EDWARD HEARTILY BIDS YOU WELCOME TO HIS CORONATION DINNER, ON JULY 5TH. 1902.

all the British monarchs of this century, he had to face the rise of the Labour Party and the radical social reforms of Lloyd George with their consequent financial toll. He died in the middle of the Parliament Bill crisis, when Asquith sought to create a regiment of new peers to force through the measure depriving the Lords of a financial veto on Parliamentary business.

Opposite Another of Edward's reputed mistresses, Sarah Bernhardt.

Below George V and his family, at Windsor. George had not expected to become king.

George V
1910-1936

Born at Marlborough House, London on June 3, 1865.

Succeeded as King of Great Britain and Ireland, and Emperor of India on May 6, 1910 at the age of 44.

Eldest surviving son of his predecessor Edward, his elder brother Albert Duke of Clarence having died in 1892.

Married on July 6, 1893, when he was 28 and she was 26, Princess May of Teck, grand-daughter of Adolphus Duke of Cambridge and daughter of Francis Duke of Teck. She survived him and died in 1953.

Children EDWARD; GEORGE; Mary, Princess Royal, Countess of Harewood, died 1965; Henry Duke of Gloucester, died 1974; George Duke of Kent died on active service 1942; John died 1919.

Died of pneumonia following general weakening, at Sandringham on January 20, 1936, at the age of 70, having reigned 25 years. Buried in St George's Chapel, Windsor.

Profile Medium height, fresh complexion, blue eyes, always bearded, short brown hair, high forehead, figure always trim, always elegantly and formally dressed. A shy man and harsh disciplinarian, enthusiastic about the navy and the Establishment, forced by a

severe sense of duty to attend to multifarious details of State. His attitude to the arts is best expressed by his dictum: 'People who write books ought to be shut up'.

᠅᠅᠅᠅᠅᠅᠅᠅᠅᠅᠅

George never expected to be king and had not been trained for the position in youth. When his elder brother, who already exhibited an extremely dissolute character, died when George was 27, this keen professional naval officer had not only to abandon the service and train for kingship, but found it his additional duty to marry the fiancée of his dead brother, Princess May of

Right *The first Christmas broadcast to the nation. They brought George enormous popular acclaim.*

Opposite *One of George V's major enthusiasms was for the Navy, in which he held the rank of captain.*

Below *The First World War darkened George's reign. Trench warfare was particularly difficult.*

KING GEORGE AS A CAPTAIN
IN HIS OWN NAVY

THIS STUDY OF OUR NEW KING WAS MADE WHILE HE WAS CAPTAIN OF H.M.S. "CRESCENT"
BY F. G. O. STUART

Teck, who had been picked for the post of future queen by the iron-hard gaze of George's grandmother Victoria.

George had an enviably easy and affectionate relationship with his father, Edward VII, in spite of Edward's wild extra-marital life which had no appeal for the son. Edward, who kept no information from him in his frequent correspondence and conversation, said they were 'like brothers'. George wrote in his diary on his accession 'I have lost my best friend and the best of fathers.

I never had a word with him in my life'. Unfortunately George was completely incapable of transmitting this ideal relationship to his own children, and his wife, who took the title Queen Mary, could not transmit affection.

As king, George dutifully tried to follow his father's political example. He surmounted the crisis of the Parliament Bill, and was almost immediately confronted with World War One, which slightly consolidated the monarchy in Great Britain whereas it exploded the

system almost everywhere else. Later the throne was relatively unwounded by the politics and social frustration of the long post-war depression. George, an austere and distant man, was persuaded to begin the series of royal Christmas addresses on the radio, an innovation which quietly increased the affection in which he was generally held, and culminated in his being astounded to the point of tears at the genuine acclamation given him before he died, on the occasion of his silver jubilee.

Edward VIII
1936

Born at White Lodge, Richmond Park on June 23, 1894.

Succeeded as 'King of Great Britain, Ireland, and the British Dominions beyond the seas, Emperor of India' on January 20, 1936 at the age of 41.

Eldest son of his predecessor George.

Abdicated on December 11, 1936, aged 42, having reigned ten months.

Married in 1937 Mrs Ernest Simpson, formerly Mrs Winfield Spencer, née Wallis Warfield, daughter of Teakle Warfield, of Boston, USA.

Children None.

Died in Paris on May 28, 1972, aged 78. Buried at Frogmore House, Windsor.

Profile Short, fair, brown eyes, clean-shaven, always slim. Very sociable, but always aware of his social superiority. A keen sportsman, a cultural lowbrow.

ोोोोोोोोोोोोो

Edward received so much flattery for his effective goodwill tours of the world as diplomatic and commercial ambassador for Great Britain, after a realistic but necessarily restrained experience of World War One, that 'Our Smiling Prince' came to the throne entirely unprepared for the disapproval he was to earn from the Establishment (i.e., the constitutional politicians, the old aristocracy, the upper echelons of the Church, and the sensitive governments of the imperial dominions). He proposed to marry a twice-divorced American lady. He was barred from giving her a rank equal to his, and energetically discouraged, as Supreme Governor of the Church of England, from any marital recognition of a divorced woman. He accordingly abdicated.

Left *Edward VIII abdicated before his coronation.*

Opposite *The Duchess of Windsor, whose status as a divorcée made her unacceptable to the Establishment.*

169

George VI
1936-1952

Born at York Cottage, Sandringham on December 14, 1895.

Succeeded as King of Great Britain and Ireland and the British Dominions beyond the seas on December 11, 1936 at the age of 40. Discontinued the title of Emperor of India in 1947.

Younger brother of his predecessor Edward.

Married in Westminster Abbey on April 26, 1923, when he was 27 and she was 22, Elizabeth Bowes-Lyon, daughter of the Earl of Strathmore and Kinghorn. She survives him.

Children ELIZABETH, Margaret.

Died of cancer at Sandringham on February 6, 1952, aged 56, having reigned 15 years. Buried at St George's Chapel, Windsor.

Profile Medium height, pale complexion, brown eyes, brown hair, clean-shaven, slim build. A speech impediment on public occasions was overcome by therapy. A timid man with an awareness of duty greatly reinforced in his application and some of his decisions by the personality of his wife. Quick-tempered, not intellectual, a specialist sportsman, very 'royal', with an insistence on the minor details of rank and precedence ranging down to the order in which medals should be worn.

George VI came unwillingly to the throne in succession to his brother, whom he had looked up to as head of the family and as sovereign. He made an arranged tour of the United States and Canada which was to prove of high importance during the ensuing World War II, and after the war further imperial tours were projected. George was the first monarch on whose behalf advisers took the concept of 'public relations' seriously. He was used as a positive instrument of appeasement and goodwill, and by good-humouredly submitting to it justified the process.

Below *King George VI and Queen Elizabeth, both keen horse racing fans, arrive at Royal Ascot.*

Opposite *A portrait of George VI, an exhibit at the National Portrait Gallery.*

Left *George VI presents the DSO to Lieutenant Commander John D Ouvry, RN. The Royal family became an emotional rallying point in World War II. The King and Queen are shown inspecting bomb damage at St Thomas' London* (below) *and Madame Tussaud's* (opposite).

A relaxed family group, gathered together at Windsor. **Back row standing left to right:** *The Earl of Snowdon; the Duke of Kent; Prince Michael of Kent; the Duke of Edinburgh; the Earl of St Andrews (elder son of the Duke of Kent); Prince Charles, the Prince of Wales; Prince Andrew; Hon Angus Ogilvy and his son, James Ogilvy* **(extreme right). Seated on chairs, left to right:** *Princess Margaret, Countess of Snowdon; the Duchess of Kent (holding Lord Nicholas Windsor, her younger son); Queen Elizabeth, the Queen Mother; Queen Elizabeth II; Princess Anne; Marina Ogilvy and her mother, Princess Alexandra.* **Seated on the floor, left to right:** *Lady Sarah Armstrong Jones; Viscount Linley (the children of Princess Margaret); Prince Edward; Lady Helen Windsor (daughter of the Duke of Kent).*

Elizabeth II
1952-

Born at 17 Bruton Street, London on April 21, 1926.

Succeeded as Queen of Great Britain and Northern Ireland and of her other Realms and Territories, Head of the Commonwealth, on February 6, 1952 aged 25.

Elder daughter of her predecessor George.

Married at Westminster Abbey on November 20, 1947, when she was 21 and he was 26, Lieutenent Philip Mountbatten, Royal Navy, son of Prince Andrew of Greece and Princess Alice, who was great-granddaughter of Queen Victoria through Princess Alice, Grand Duchess of Hesse and Victoria, Princess of Battenberg, Marchioness of Milford Haven.

Children Charles, Anne, Andrew, Edward.

Left As Colonel-in-Chief of all seven regiments of the Household Guards, Queen Elizabeth takes the salute during the Trooping the Colour Ceremony.

Below Flanked by her bishops, the young queen is crowned at Westminster Abbey, 1953.

Opposite above and below As Princess Elizabeth, the Queen took her war duties seriously.

Left *Sister princesses attending a concert for children at Westminster, November 1945.*

Below and **Opposite** *As ambassadors abroad, the royal family have evolved a very special function. They are seen here visiting Auku in the Pacific (**below**) and New Zealand (**opposite**).*

178

Left *The combination of ceremony and informality achieved in the last few years is aptly demonstrated here, where a smiling queen walks alongside Charles, newly invested as Prince of Wales.*

Opposite *A dramatic photograph of the Queen wearing the Order of the Garter at Windsor Castle, June 17, 1974.*

Below *The young royals await the arrival of the Queen of Denmark. On the right is Captain Mark Phillips, husband of Princess Anne.*

Index

THE MONARCHS OF ENGLAND AND THE UNITED KINGDOM